ANDALUSIAN
COOKING

RECIPES, TYPICAL PRODUCTS, WINES, CHEESES, LIQUORS

AN APPETIZING
JOURNEY THROUGH
THE SPECIALTIES
OF A UNIQUE LAND

BONECHI

HOW TO READ THE CARDS

DIFFICULTY	FLAVOR	NUTRITIONAL VALUE
● Easy ●● Moderate ●●● Difficult	● Mild ●● Distinctive ●●● Hearty, spicy	● Low ●● Medium ●●● High

Preparation and cooking times are shown in hours (h) and minutes (e. g. 30′ is 30 minutes).

Publication created and designed by: Casa Editrice Bonechi
Editorial management: Alberto Andreini
Coordination: Paolo Piazzesi
Graphic design: Andrea Agnorelli *and* Maria Rosanna Malagrinò
Cover: Andrea Agnorelli
Video pagemaking: Andrea Agnorelli
Video pagemaking for the English edition: Studio Grafico Vanni Berti
Editing: Patrizia Chirichigno

Translation: Paula Boomsliter

In the kitchen: Lisa Mugnai
Nutritionist: Dr. John Luke Hili

The photographs relative to the recipes are property of the Casa Editrice Bonechi
photographic archives and were taken by Andrea Fantauzzo.

The other photographs used in this publication are property of the Casa Editrice Bonechi
photographic archives and were taken by Luigi Di Giovine, Andrea Fantauzzo, *and* Paolo Giambone.

*The publisher apologizes in advance for any unintentional omissions and would be pleased
to insert the appropriate acknowledgements in any subsequent edition of this publication.*

© Copyright 2003
by CASA EDITRICE BONECHI - Florence - Italy
E-mail: bonechi@bonechi.it   Internet: www.bonechi.it

Printed in Italy by Centro Stampa Editoriale Bonechi.

ISBN 88-476-1285-3

***

EIGHT TIMES ONE

Blossoming Andalusia, the extreme southern limb of the Iberian pentagon, a three-fold miracle of beauty: splendid beaches, a fertile countryside furrowed by rivers, and high mountains ringed with woodlands, with blue lakes and snow-capped peaks, wild lands protected as natural parks. Bathed on the east by the Mediterranean and on the west by the Atlantic, Andalusia is considered by some a compendium of Spain that summarizes the country's vocation for seafaring on two fronts, the austerity of the pasturelands, the serenity of the rural life, the ancient Greek and Latin matrix, and a willingness to embrace the new. Punta Marroquí reaches out toward Africa, almost as if to point out the region's calling as the irreplaceable ambassador of the refined civilizations of other continents, to the benefit of Europe. But Andalusia is above all itself, a world apart, a universe of cultures, traditions, customs, and flavors. Each of its eight provinces, gathered around the administrative center Seville, goes proud of its own peculiar identity.

The geographical and anthropological variety of the region is reflected in the cuisine and the gastronomy, regaling us with a wide selection of dishes and ingredients. But we must not forget: Andalusian cooking is multiform, not heterogeneous; although it reflects different territories, peoples, and life styles, it is in substance unitary. The common denominator is sincerity, the intrinsic value of a frugal but tasty, measured but imaginative board that succeeds in bringing out the best in the foods themselves—without foregoing a touch of magic. An ancient yet always new style of cooking that has remained true to its own lights even despite the changes induced by the new invasion of tourists, thanks in large part to the traditional skill of the Andalusian people in valorizing the genuine products of a generous land. As you will see in the section dedicated to typical products, Andalusia gives us excellent processed pork products and delicious cheeses, produces great quantities of choice vegetables and exquisite fruit, presses many top-quality olive oils, and boasts magnificent wines, first and foremost the famous nectars of Jerez.

For a long time, Andalusian cuisine was, we might say, overshadowed by other schools of Iberian cooking, above all the Catalan and the Galician, which are better known abroad and of prevalently European, and sometimes even Nordic, matrix. But thanks to progressive valorization of the Mediterranean diet, it has won back the place in the sun it merits. The variety deriving from the multifaceted conformation of the territory is one reason why Andalusian gastronomy is different from that of every other region of Spain, but its differentiation also reflects the alternation, interaction, and mutual contamination of very different cultures. In Andalusian gastronomy, well-defined Mediterranean characteristics intertwine with continental echoes, the customs of the Spanish gypsies, the legacies of the Sephardite Jews, and above all the complex and elegant Arab culinary tradition, which in turn is permeated with myriad exotic influences. As we know, the Arab influence is more evident in Andalusia than in the other regions of Spain that were also Moorish kingdoms, both because of the duration of the domination (begun in the 8th century and lasting until the end of the 15th) and because of the conquerors' conscientious management of this land. They fecundated the culture, bridging the region not only to the Islamic kingdoms of Africa but also to Arabia, Persia, and India, refined civilizations with extraordinary gastronomic skill inspired by avant-garde medical and scientific knowledge; from Africa and the Orient there came not only ingredients but also techniques, ideas, and styles. It is to the that Arabs we attribute the merit for having imported rice, which is still cultivated in some parts of Andalusia, and the eggplant, native to India, which has probably been cultivated in Andalusia since the 9th century; and for having incentivated cultivation of asparagus and artichokes. The Arabs also introduced culinary use of many varieties of spices (cinnamon, cloves, coriander, turmeric, Persian cumin, ginger, nutmeg, sesame, and many others), the taste for fruit sherbets and syrups, and the use of honey, dates, and almonds in sweets, as we see in the

are sometimes the very same that are pressed to produce the excellent oil for the vinaigrette dressing made with a touch of aromatic vinegar. The appetizers and salads are usually considered fresh invitations, appealing starters for launching a meal, but they also may be transformed into all-in-one dishes for summer meals.

A close relative of the salads is the world-famous gazpacho, the Andalusian national dish even before the arrival of the Arabs and above all well before the tomato was imported from the New World. The formula associates the mixed fresh vegetables, the fine oil, and the excellent vinegar that have

In Andalusia, nature, tradition, and art reveal their true essences:
the famous beaches of the Costa del Sol, the passionate vitality of the gypsy population. Bottom, the polychrome statue of Isabella of Castile and, on the preceding page, a detail of the Patio de los Leones in the Alhambra in Granada.

Arab-Andalusian recipes in a text by an unknown author written during the prosperous times of the Almohad dynasty, which in the 11th century replaced the Almoravids, and in the Fadhalat al-Jiwan compendium produced by Ibn Razin al-Tujibi between the 13th and 14th centuries.

The mixing of so many influences, nature's benevolence, and Andalusian skill thus gave rise to a style of cooking of incredible richness and variety, possessing its own unmistakable character in which the principal element is generosity, as you will see as you follow us on this journey through its specialties on an itinerary laid out to propose the best. We begin with the *tapas*, appetizing morsels—whether kebabs of fish or the products of the land, in the Berber style, or flavorful anchovies and marinated vegetables, or fresh crustaceans—that provide a lighthearted pretext for sipping the excellent dry white wines of Jerez and Córdoba, unequalled for preparing the palate for the dishes of this noble cuisine. Alongside the *tapas* we have the imaginative, multicolored salads, like the *pipirrana* or the *remojón* made with bitter oranges, which are very common in Andalusia, given the quality and the abundance of tomatoes, peppers, and delicious table olives—which

never been lacking in Andalusia since Roman times. The next course in any Andalusian menu is the soup, and since there are almost an infinite number of types among which to choose we will have to make do with a few of the best. We will begin with delectable dishes fragrant with garlic, like the *sopa de gato*, and go on to hearty recipes based on rice, like the *sopa de Granada*, or on legumes, like the *sopa de lentejas rojas* or the *berza gitana*; nor must we forget the delicious, traditional, and elegant seafood and fish dishes like the *gazpachuelo*, the *sopa de galeras*, the *caldo de perro*, and the *sopa "Viña AB."*

And now on to the entrées. While the recipes based on pork—the prized *cerdo ibérico*—or beef and veal, like the *lomo a la malagueña*, basted with good Málaga wine, or the *estofado a la andaluza* are simply delicious, the genuine flavors of this land are probably best expressed by the lamb and kid dishes, enlivened by the intense fragrance of the herbs, or by the recipes based on "white" meats and game birds and game, with their strong Arabian reminiscences, ennobled by the pungent aroma of Andalusian vinegar and enriched with succulent, mild-flavored olives.

The richness of the dishes on the Andalusian board doubles when we speak of fish and seafood, since they count on both the Atlantic fishing grounds and the generosity of the Mediterranean Sea. The ports and the markets are carnivals of white-fleshed and "blue" fishes, anchovies and sardines, mullets and sole; the swordfish and tuna that pass the Strait of Gibraltar end up in memorable dishes like the *pez espada a la malagueña* and the *atún rojo marinado*. From the wharves of the Costa del Sol and Cádiz store come mollusks and crustaceans, shrimp of all sizes, mantis prawns, spiny and European lobsters, mussels, clams, and an infinity of others. All this for a thousand seafood recipes

that solomonically valorize the varieties of fish found in both waters, often quite different, often relying on the exotic enchantment of spices—even though, all told, the most authentically Andalusian dish is probably the totally uncomplicated *pescaíto frito*, a crisp fry of mixed small fish. The fine local white wines are a noble accompaniment to the seafood dishes, but are also quite often transformed into a precious ingredient, as in the recipe for *dorada al Jerez*. Nor is there any lack of flavorful recipes based on fresh or salt cod, like the delectable *andrajos de Jaén*.

After dedicating ample space to egg dishes, omnipresent on the Andalusian table, cooked with vegetables and sausages to make hearty all-in-one dishes (like the deliciously rich *huevos a la flamenca*), we pay homage to the all-round goodness of Andalusian vegetables and legumes with recipes that are unequalled for simplicity and flavor. And finally, as in any self-respecting meal, we go on to cakes and desserts: once again, we have taken the best there is (among the recipes that lend themselves to preparation in the home kitchen). Many of the desserts show clear and profound Arab influences (even though, despite their Islamic origin, these delicacies are perfect accompanied by the superb Andalusian dessert wines) in the honey, spices, almonds, and raisins that so often figure among the ingredients. Another very important

Sevilla: the Salón de los Embajadores in the Alcázar and a Roman archeological find brought to light at the excavations at Itálica, near the city.

theme is that of the kitchens of the convents, from which come elaborate preparations based on simple, homely ingredients: Seville is famous for the *yemas* invented in the monasteries of Saint Leander and Saint Ursula, tender sugar-glazed egg-yolk balls aromatized with cinnamon and lemon.

The Arab influence is particularly evident in the desserts of Córdoba and above all of Granada, with the *almendrados* and the *soplillos*, in which the solar, velvety flavor of almonds predominates, and the *roscos* fragrant with anise; or yet again, in the rich *bollos*, delicious *cuajanos*, *tocinillos de cielo* of golden egg custard covered with dark caramel. The Catholic tradition reappears in the curious *piononos* of Santa Fe, which with the white of the meringue and the yellow of the custard recall the Vatican flag. In Seville we find the *mostachones*, spiced honey *rosquillos* with a Moorish flavor, flaky *bizcochos*, *tortas de aceite* that enclose in a mantle of glaze a pastry dignified by the golden caress of Andalusian oil, *polvorones* ennobled with lard and sugar-glazed. Our proposals include desserts based on rice (*arroz con leche*) or rich in custard (*brazo de gitano*) or even soaked in excellent Andalusian wine (*borrachuelos* and *pastel de piñones*).

A NOTE ON INGREDIENTS

Most of our recipes, especially those that are somewhat complicated, are illustrated with step-by-step photographs to better explain preparation. We suggest first reading the list of ingredients carefully, along with the information on preparation and cooking times, the level of difficulty, the more or less accentuated flavor, and nutritional content, and then reading through the entire recipe before beginning. And, as usual . . . bon appetit!

A technical detail: the expression "ground hot red pepper," whether it appears in the lists of ingredients or in the text of the recipes, means Spanish *pimentón*, a spice (not necessarily very hot) obtained by drying and grinding *Capsicum annuum* peppers, which are fiery red in color and strongly flavored. The types found in Andalusia, as in all of Spain, are either *fuerte* or *dulce* (hot or mild); your choice will depend on your tastes and eating habits. The *pimentón* is a true ingredient, indispensable for the success of the recipe, and not just a "touch" added to make the dishes more appetizing. In some English-speaking countries this ingredient is erroneously called paprika: it is not the Hungarian paprika, which is derived from a species of pepper of Indian origin, with smaller fruits and a more pungent aroma; *pimentón* is made with New World species of peppers. In any case, even though it is different as regards flavor, color, and gastronomic value, mild or hot paprika may be used as a surrogate for *pimentón*, as may be the ground chilies and pimientos sold in natural produce shops.

Other information on typically Andalusian ingredients and products, beginning with the famous Jabugo hams, will be found in the section on typical products and in the notes that accompany the recipes in which they are ingredients.

A WORD FROM THE NUTRITIONIST

*A*ndalusian cooking respects the nutritional principles of that way of preparing foods and of eating we define as the "Mediterranean diet," known throughout the world for its capacity to help prevent illnesses like strokes and heart attacks. As we all know, this style of nutrition is based on carbohydrates; in Andalusia, these are the derivates of durum wheat flour and rice, bread, and

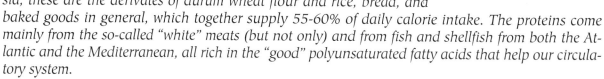

baked goods in general, which together supply 55-60% of daily calorie intake. The proteins come mainly from the so-called "white" meats (but not only) and from fish and shellfish from both the Atlantic and the Mediterranean, all rich in the "good" polyunsaturated fatty acids that help our circulatory system.

Legumes appear frequently on the menu, especially in the "all-in-one" dishes. They supply proteins of lesser biological value but in exchange contain great quantities of fiber, which help keep down cholesterol and triglyceride levels and prevent constipation. Fats are

for the most part supplied by extra virgin olive oil, which with its monounsaturated fat reinforces the action of the polyunsaturates just mentioned.

Cooked and raw vegetables are another everyday menu item that makes a daily contribution of at least 25 grams of fiber to our organism. Finally, Andalusian cooking makes ample use of typically Mediterranean flavorings and many spices that are the "legacy" of Arab domination.

CONTENTS

The interior of the Mezquita-Catedral of Córdoba. On the facing page, a modern azulejo.

THE RECIPES

Granada: the Patio de los Arrayanes with the Comares tower, in the 13th-century Alcazaba, the oldest portion of the Alhambra.

Hors d'œuvre and Salads

*To accompany your aperitif,
as you chat while waiting to sit down to dinner,
to prepare the palate for more "weighty" courses.
Welcome to the brightly-colored, stimulating,
and seemingly boundless world of Andalusia's appetizers,
rich in pleasing surprises,
that keep company with fresh and appetizing salads . . .*

1

BERENJENAS Y CALABAZA CON SALSA DE VINAGRE

Eggplant and Squash with Vinegar Sauce

1 large eggplant
250 g/½ lb squash,
  in a single piece
3 cloves garlic
Anise, coriander, and cumin
  (seeds)
1 envelope powdered saffron
Malaga raisins
Red wine vinegar
Coarse salt, table salt,
  and pepper
Olive oil

Servings: 4	
Preparation time: 20'+30'	
Cooking time: 20'	
Difficulty: ●●	
Flavor: ●●●	
Kcal (per serving): 170	
Protein (per serving): 3	
Fat (per serving): 10	
Nutritional value: ●●	

Rinse the eggplant, peel, and cut into thick slices (about 1.5 cm/ ½ inch). Lay the slices on a tray, sprinkle with coarse salt, and allow to stand, weighted, for about ½ hour until the moisture is squeezed out. At the same time, place a handful of raisins in water to soak. Blanch the squash in lightly-salted boiling water, drain well, peel, and cut into 1.5 cm/½ inch dice. Rinse the eggplant slices under cold running water, dry, and cut into 1.5 cm/½ inch cubes.

Sauté the diced eggplant and squash, until golden, over high heat in a skillet with 4-5 tablespoons oil. Add the drained and squeezed raisins, a teaspoon of coriander seeds, and the saffron; continue to cook for 3-4 minutes. Add 2-3 tablespoons vinegar, lower the flame, and allow the flavors to blend while mixing constantly. Serve the vegetables as an appetizer, with on the side a dressing made with 1 cup lukewarm oil emulsified with 2-3 tablespoons vinegar and sprinkled with anise and cumin seeds. Invite your guests to help themselves to the vegetable cubes with toothpicks, and to dunk them in the dressing.

BROCHETAS DE ALMERÍA

Mixed Marinated Kebabs

500 g/1 lb 2 oz lean pork,
  chicken, or beef
  (in one, firm piece)
180 g/¹/₂ lb smoked bacon
2-3 spring onions
2 salad tomatoes
1 yellow bell pepper
3-4 slices bakery bread,
  with crusts removed, diced

For the marinade:
Pine nuts (about ¹/₃ cup)
Ground cinnamon, nutmeg,
  and saffron
Parsley (one sprig)
Dry white wine
Salt and freshly ground pepper
Olive oil

Servings: 8	
Preparation time: 20'+3-4h	
Cooking time: 7-10'	
Difficulty: ●	
Flavor: ● ●	
Kcal (per serving): 709	
Protein (per serving): 20	
Fat (per serving): 50	
Nutritional value: ● ● ●	

1 Pound the pine nuts to a paste in a mortar, add ¹/₂ teaspoon ground cinnamon, a pinch of grated nutmeg, and one envelope powdered saffron. Rub this paste delicately all over the meat and place in a bowl to marinate with the chopped parsley, 1 cup white wine and 4-5 tablespoons oil. Turn the meat every now and then. In the meantime, wash and prepare the vegetables: cut the spring onions into regular-sized pieces, and the tomatoes and the pepper (having removed the seeds and fibrous parts) into small triangles.

2 After 3-4 hours, drain the meat (reserve the marinade liquid) and cube. Trim the rind off the bacon before cutting it. On long skewers, alternate pieces of meat and bacon with bits of onion, triangles of tomato and pepper, and cubes of bread. Sprinkle with salt and place on a hot grill for 6-7 minutes, turning once a minute until browned on all sides and basting with the marinade liquid. As an alternative, place the skewers in a large ovenproof dish, brush with some of the marinade liquid, and cook in a hot oven (220°C/400-425°F) for 10 minutes. Baste as necessary. Serve piping hot sprinkled with freshly ground pepper.

ESCABECHE DE BOQUERONES

Marinated Anchovies ▶

1 kg/2 1/4 lbs fresh anchovies
4-5 cloves garlic
Bay leaves
Cumin, fennel seeds,
    and ground ginger
Saffron (whole stigmas)
40 g/5 tbsp flour
2.5 dl/1 1/4 cups (ca.)
    red wine vinegar
Salt and peppercorns
Oil for frying
Olive oil

Servings: 6-8	
Preparation time: 30'+24h	
Cooking time: 20'	
Difficulty: ● ●	
Flavor: ● ● ●	
Kcal (per serving): 618	
Protein (per serving): 34	
Fat (per serving): 49	
Nutritional value: ● ● ●	

1 Clean the anchovies, removing the heads, bones, entrails, and tails. Do not separate the fillets along the dorsal side. Open the fish and flatten; rinse under cold running water. Dry, flour, and fry in deep hot oil; drain and allow to dry on paper towels. Salt moderately.

2 In a skillet, sauté the garlic cloves with 2-3 tablespoons oil until softened: lift out and drain. Pound the garlic to a smooth paste in a mortar with a pinch of salt, a good-sized pinch of saffron stigmas, and about 1/4 teaspoons each cumin seeds and ground ginger. Dilute the paste with the vinegar. Layer the fried anchovies in a terrine, dorsal side down; top with 2 bay leaves. Mix a cup of water with the spice-and-vinegar mixture and pour it over the fish to just cover. Seal the terrine with aluminum foil and refrigerate for at least 24 hours. Serve as an appetizer.

REMOJÓN

Bitter Orange Salad

2 bitter oranges
250 g/8 oz oil-packed
    mackerel fillets
50 g/2 oz green olives, pitted
2 spring onions
1 tomato
1 clove garlic
Coriander leaves (for garnish)
Jerez vinegar
Toasted bread rounds
    (optional, for serving)
Salt and pepper
Olive oil

Servings: 4-6	
Preparation time: 20'+1h	
Difficulty: ●	
Flavor: ● ●	
Kcal (per serving): 374	
Protein (per serving): 14	
Fat (per serving): 21	
Nutritional value: ● ● ●	

Rinse the tomato, cut open, seed, and dice. Wash and trim the onions (removing the green tips) and peel the garlic; cut both into very thin rounds. Peel the oranges and carefully remove all the white inner skin. Separate the sections of 1 1/2 oranges and cut into small pieces. In a serving bowl, mix the orange pieces with the well-drained and broken-up mackerel filets, the garlic, the onions, the olives, and the tomato. Mix all the salad ingredients well and—especially in the summertime—allow to cool for an hour in the refrigerator. At serving time, dress the salad with salt, pepper, oil, and a drop of vinegar. Serve as is or on rounds of toasted bread, garnished with the remaining 1/2 orange, sliced thinly, and coriander leaves. As an alternative to the mackerel, try oil-packed tuna or grilled and finely-crumbled desalted salt cod.

1

2

TORTILLITAS DE CAMARONES A LA GADITANA

Shrimp Fritters

1 Peel the onion and chop it finely with the seeded *pimiento*. Put into a bowl and add the chopped parsley and the shrimp (rinsed, dried, and broken into pieces). Mix well.

2 Add the flour, about ½ cup wine, the yeast, and sufficient cold water (about 4 dl/1½-2 cups) to make a fairly stiff batter. Beat with a whisk or mixer. Let stand for 2-3 hours in a cool place.

3 Taking a tablespoon of batter at a time, drop the *tortillitas* into very hot oil. Fry, turning with a slotted spoon, until golden all over.

4 As soon as they are ready, remove from the oil one at a time and drain; dry on paper towels on a serving dish. Sprinkle sparingly with salt and serve hot.

The impressive and quite singular Mezquita-Catedral of Córdoba: after the Reconquista, the mosque built in the year 786 by the Arabs became a Catholic place of worship and in 1523 the city's cathedral.

		Servings: 4
200 g/6 oz shrimp tails, shelled	Parsley	Preparation time: 15'+3h
1 medium-sized onion	Salt	Cooking time: 15'
250 g/2 cups flour	Oil for frying	Difficulty: ● ●
15 g/¹/₂ oz compressed yeast (about 1 cake)		Flavor: ● ●
1 red *pimiento*		Kcal (per serving): 557
Dry white wine		Protein (per serving): 14
		Fat (per serving): 26
		Nutritional value: ● ● ●

PIPIRRANA Y PORRA ANTEQUERANA

Mixed Salad Antequera Style

For the *porra:*
2-3 slices bakery bread (with crusts removed)
2 ripe tomatoes
2 bell peppers
4 cloves garlic

For the *pipirrana:*
2 ripe tomatoes
2 bell peppers
2 spring onions
1 clove garlic
1 egg

6 eggs
Vinegar
Salt
Olive oil

Servings: 6-8
Preparation time: 20'+30'
Cooking time: 7'
Difficulty: ●
Flavor: ●●●
Kcal (per serving): 348
Protein (per serving): 15
Fat (per serving): 20
Nutritional value: ●●●

Boil all the eggs for 7 minutes; cool and shell. To make the *porra*, first sprinkle the bread slices with water to dampen but not overly wet them. Clean and trim the tomatoes and peppers; remove the seeds and the white membranes. In a food mill, blend with the peeled garlic and the bread until soft and spongy. Transfer to a bowl and incorporate the oil, the vinegar, and a pinch of salt. Allow to stand while preparing the *pipirrana*. Prepare the tomatoes and peppers as described above, then chop as finely as possible. Place in a small bowl with the onions (peeled, trimmed, and cut into rounds), the finely-chopped garlic, the chopped white of one hard-boiled egg, and a pinch of salt. In a mortar, pound the yolk of the hard-boiled egg and work in enough oil and vinegar to obtain a dressing for the salad.

Serve with hard-boiled egg rounds (the *porra* is spread and the *pipirrana* piled on the egg rounds) as a tasty appetizer.

The porra
is a specialty
of Antequera, a
town near Málaga:
it is also a popular
dish in Córdoba,
where it goes
by the name of
salmorejo. The
pipirrana, *made
in greater quantity
and with drained
oil-packed tuna
or cubed salt-cured
ham added,
is an excellent
summertime first
course, served cold,
or a side dish to be
served at room
temperature.*

Soups
and
First Courses

Mar, sierra y campaña:
the traditional Andalusian first courses
reflect the three faces of a generous land.
Delicate fragrances from the sea,
the strong flavors of the processed meats
that corroborate cabbage and legumes,
the solar naturalness of gazpacho,
a food and a cooler rolled into one.
For the peace of mind of our dogs and cats,
it is worthwhile stressing that the caldo de perro
and the sopa de gato do NOT include
our household pets among the ingredients . . .

2

CALDO DE PERRO

Cod Soup with Orange

500 g/1 lb cod fillets
1 onion
2-3 cloves garlic
2 bitter oranges (or 3 sweet
   oranges and 1 lemon)
Vegetable stock
   (made with bouillon cubes),
   ca. 2 liters/8 cups
Salt
Olive oil

Servings: 4	
Preparation time: 10'+2h	
Cooking time: 20'	
Difficulty: ●●	
Flavor: ●●●	
Kcal (per serving): 328	
Protein (per serving): 24	
Fat (per serving): 21	
Nutritional value: ●●●	

Lay the cod fillets on a plate, sprinkle with salt, cover, and allow to stand for about 2 hours. Sauté the garlic cloves until golden with 5-6 tablespoons oil; as soon as they color, lift them out with a skimmer and replace with the peeled and finely-minced onion. Cook over low heat until softened (3-4 minutes), then add the hot stock (in truth, the traditional recipe calls simply for hot water) and cover. Simmer until the onion is falling apart. If the volume of the cooking liquid should decrease considerably during cooking, add more stock. Add the rinsed cod fillets, check the salt (you should need to add very little, if any), cover again and simmer for about 5 minutes. Remove the fish, drain, break into small pieces, and distribute in individual serving bowls. Ladle stock into each bowl and pour a dash of bitter orange juice into each. The *caldo de perro* (literally, "dog broth") is now ready to enjoy—even though no one knows what it has to do with canines!

BERZA GITANA

Vegetable Soup with Meat

Soak the chickpeas and beans for 6 hours before beginning. To start, prepare the vegetables (including the *tagarninas*): wash and trim each as suitable. Singe the pig's cheek, tail, and foot; scrape, rinse, and dry. Split the foot in two and place in a large soup pot with the cheek and tail, the drained chickpeas, and about 2 liters/8 cups cold, lightly salted water. Light the burner, cover the pan, and bring to a slow boil. Cook for about 30 minutes and then add the beans and the pork meat cut into bite-size pieces. Simmer, covered, for another 30 minutes. Add the cabbage (cut into wedges), the *tagarninas* and the celery (diced), the *chorizo*, and 1 tablespoon *pimentón*. Cover again and simmer for 1 hour. Lastly, add the *morcilla*, adjust the salt, and continue cooking for another half hour or more. Uncover the pot and add the *manteca colorá*; allow it to melt slowly, then return the pot to the boil and turn off the burner. Cut the sausages and the cheek, foot, and tail meat into pieces and serve the *berza* piping hot.

500 g/1 lb Savoy cabbage
150 g/5-6 oz dried chickpeas
150 g/5-6 oz dried *alubias* beans
150 g/5-6 oz *tagarninas*
  (see note)
1 stalk celery
200 g/$\frac{1}{2}$ lb lean pork meat
  (boned)
100 g/$\frac{1}{4}$ lb pork cheek (or ear)
1 pig's foot and 1 tail
100 g/$\frac{1}{4}$ lb *chorizo* (see p. 87)
100 g/$\frac{1}{4}$ lb *morcilla* (see p. 87)
Pimentón dulce
  (or sweet paprika)
Salt
100 g/$\frac{1}{4}$ lb *manteca colorá*
  (see note)

Servings: 6	
Preparation time: 20'+6h	
Cooking time: 3h	
Difficulty: ● ●	
Flavor: ● ●	
Kcal (per serving): 684	
Protein (per serving): 26	
Fat (per serving): 48	
Nutritional value: ● ● ●	

Manteca colorá, *a commonly-used ingredient in Andalusia, is extra-fine emulsified lard with* pimentón.

Tagarninas, *instead, are the slender stems of a variety of wild cardoon, gathered in the fields and used frequently in* traditional cooking. A good substitute, weight-for-weight, is common cardoon cut into strips and held in acidulated water until the moment of use. The berza may be enriched with potatoes, squash, or green beans.

Sevilla's Real Plaza de la Maestranza, the beautiful and world-renowned plaza de toros.

GAZPACHUELO

Turbot Soup with Mayonnaise

Turbot, ca. 600 g/1 ¼ lbs
500 g (1 lb 2 oz) potatoes
300 g (12 oz or 1 ¼ cups)
   mayonnaise (see note)
1 stalk celery
1 bay leaf
1 sprig parsley
Red wine vinegar
Salt

Servings: 4	
Preparation time: 25′	
Cooking time: 35′	
Difficulty: ●●	
Flavor: ●	
Kcal (per serving): 798	
Protein (per serving): 28	
Fat (per serving): 62	
Nutritional value: ●●●	

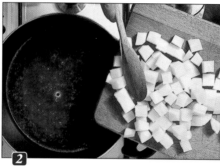

1 Gut, skin, and fillet the turbot, reserving the head, tail, fins, and bones; put them into a pan with about 1 liter (4 cups) cold water, the trimmed and sliced celery, the sprig of parsley, the bay leaf, and a pinch of salt. Bring to a boil, cover, lower the heat, and simmer gently for 15 minutes.

2 In the meantime, peel the potatoes, rinse, dry, and cut into cubes. Strain the fish stock (fumet) through a fine sieve (eliminating all solid parts) into a soup pot. Add the potatoes.

Mayonnaise, the pride of French cuisine, is believed by some experts on the matter to have originated in Spain. To make the quantity required for this recipe, place two egg yolks in a bowl with a pinch of salt. Pour in a drop of oil (in all, you'll need about 1 1/2 cups for 2 large yolks) and begin beating with a wire whisk or wooden spoon. Take care always to beat in the same direction. Beat in the oil very slowly, a few drops at a time; when the sauce begins to thicken, relax! When all the oil has been added, beat in the juice of 1 lemon (or 2-3 tablespoons vinegar). You can also make mayonnaise with an electric mixer set to medium speed.

3 Slowly bring the stock to a boil again and simmer for about 15 minutes. Cut the fish into rectangular pieces and lay gently in the soup. Simmer over low heat for a further five minutes, tasting for salt.

4 With a slotted spoon or skimmer, remove the fish and the potatoes to a soup tureen. Allow the broth to cool slightly, then pour it into a bowl and blend in the prepared mayonnaise very delicately. Pour the mixture over the fish and potatoes. Add 2 tablespoons wine vinegar, stir gently, and serve.

SOPA DE GALERAS

Prawn Soup

1 kg/2 ¼ lbs fresh mantis
  prawns
2 onions
1 clove garlic
Parsley
8 slices bakery bread, toasted
Salt
Olive oil

Servings:	4
Preparation time:	10'
Cooking time:	15'
Difficulty:	●
Flavor:	● ●
Kcal (per serving):	492
Protein (per serving):	19
Fat (per serving):	12
Nutritional value:	● ● ●

Rinse the prawns and blanch in lightly salted boiling water for 1 minute. Drain, transfer to a platter, and keep warm. Strain and reserve the cooking liquid.

Peel the onions and the garlic. Mince finely and sauté slowly with 4-5 tablespoons oil for 3-4 minutes. Add the prawn cooking liquid, cover, and simmer for 10 minutes. Arrange the toasted bread slices in individual serving dishes, top with the prawns, and bathe with the broth. Sprinkle with finely-minced fresh parsley and serve.

The delicate *sopa de galeras* is best in the winter months, when the prawns are meatier and filled with their "coral" (roe).

GAZPACHO

1 Wash all the vegetables well; peel the cucumber and dice finely; peel the tomatoes and cut into tiny cubes; slice the onions into thin rings; prepare the pepper by removing the seeds and white fibrous parts, and chop. Put all these ingredients into a bowl; add the crushed cloves of garlic and the finely crumbled slice of crustless bread. Add a tablespoon of red vinegar, one of olive oil, and a pinch of salt. Mix well.

2 Transfer the mixture to a food mixer (according to the quantity being prepared, this step may have to be repeated several times) and blend to obtain a smooth and creamy consistency; taste for salt, adjusting if necessary. Refrigerate for about 2 hours before serving. Garnish the gazpacho at will and serve accompanied by slices or strips of toasted bread. For a spicier flavor, add a pinch of ground *pimiento* to the vegetables in the food mixer.

6 ripe tomatoes
1 cucumber
1 sweet pepper
2 spring onions
2-3 cloves garlic
4-6 slices bakery bread
  + 1 slice with crust removed
Red wine vinegar
Salt
Olive oil

Servings: 4	
Preparation time: 20'+2h	
Difficulty: ●	
Flavor: ● ●	
Kcal (per serving): 327	
Protein (per serving): 8	
Fat (per serving): 4	
Nutritional value: ●	

SOPA DE GATO

Garlic Soup

5-6 slices day-old bakery bread
1 head garlic
Ground hot red pepper
   (*pimentón*)
Vegetable stock
   (made with bouillon cubes),
   1.5 liters/6 cups
Aged cheese for grating
   (see note)
Salt and pepper, olive oil

Servings: 4	
Preparation time: 20'	
Cooking time: 35'	
Difficulty: ●●	
Flavor: ●●●	
Kcal (per serving): 450	
Protein (per serving): 15	
Fat (per serving): 20	
Nutritional value: ●●	

Dice the bread.
Fry the croutons over medium heat in 4-5 tablespoons oil, turning often, until uniformly golden (2-3 minutes). Add the peeled and minced cloves of the head of garlic, 1 teaspoon ground hot red pepper, the stock, and salt and pepper to taste. Cover the pan and simmer for about 20 minutes. In the meantime, preheat the oven to 200 °C/375-400°F. Portion the *sopa* into individual-serving ovenproof bowls and bake for about 10 minutes. Sprinkle generously with grated cheese and serve immediately.

As you can see, the "cat" in the title does not appear in the recipe. Might it have originated to placate dog-lovers' reactions to the title caldo de perro?
If you do not have aged manchego (or mahón) cheese, Italian Parmigiano-Reggiano is a good substitute.

Sopa "Viña AB"

Fish Soup with Jerez Wine

200 g/¹⁄₂ lb angler fish
200 g/¹⁄₂ lb cod fillets
500 g/1 ¹⁄₄ lbs clams (soaked to rid them of sand)
200 g/¹⁄₂ lb peeled prawn tails
250 g/8 oz mayonnaise (pre-prepared)
1 ripe tomato
1 leek
1 onion
2 cloves garlic
Bay leaves and parsley
"Viña AB" brand Jerez *fino* wine (or other brand, or other dry white wine), 1.5 dl/ ca. ²⁄₃ cup (see pp. 92-95)
1 lemon
Salt

Servings: 6	
Preparation time: 20'	
Cooking time: 30'	
Difficulty: ● ● ●	
Flavor: ● ●	
Kcal (per serving): 482	
Protein (per serving): 20	
Fat (per serving): 34	
Nutritional value: ● ●	

Clean and trim the vegetables. Drop the angler fish and the cod into 2 liters/2 quarts lightly-salted boiling water; after 5 minutes, add the prawn tails. Boil 5 minutes longer, then drain the fish and shellfish, reserving the stock. Keep the shellfish warm while carefully cleaning the fish: skin, bone, and remove all cartilage, fins, etc. (reserve these parts). Hold the cleaned fish warm with the shellfish. Place the soaked clams in a flat pan with a little water and set over low heat until they open. Shuck the clams. Strain the cooking liquor into another pot with the strained fish stock. Bring to a slow boil, add the fish bones and scraps, the leek cut into rounds, the onion cut into wedges, the peeled garlic, and the diced tomato, a bay leaf, and a small bunch of parsley. Cook for 15 minutes, then filter the fumet through a fine strainer and return to the pot. Add the wine, the clams, and the mayonnaise tempered in a ladleful of hot soup. Stir until well mixed, then add the fish, cut into bite-size pieces, and the shellfish. Heat to just below boiling. Serve the soup hot with a few drops of lemon juice.

A wine-cellar with casks stacked pyramid-fashion.

This dish, today found throughout Andalusia, originated in Málaga. The chef of the "La Alegría" restaurant—who unfortunately died some years ago—had decided to surprise his loyal customers by adding a dash of "Viña AB" Jerez wine to his already delicately exquisite fish soup. It was such a success that the soup was immediately renamed for the wine. If you prefer not using prepared mayonnaise, make your own with one or two eggs following the instructions given on page 20.

SOPA DE GRANADA

Vegetable Soup with Meatballs

1 Set the lentils to soak an hour or two before beginning. In a mortar, grind a piece of cinnamon, $1/2$ teaspoon coriander seeds, and 3-4 peppercorns. In a bowl, mix the ground meat with the beaten egg, the mortar-ground spices, and a pinch of salt. Shape into small balls and flour lightly. Fry in a skillet with a little hot oil until golden; drain on paper towels and keep warm.

2 Trim the spinach and wash thoroughly to eliminate all traces of sand and dirt; drain without drying. Chop the onion and cook (a terracotta pot with a cover is best) uncovered with 4-5 tablespoons oil until soft. Add the rice, the drained lentils, 2 liters/8 cups hot water, and a pinch of salt.

3 Cover the pot and simmer for 10 minutes. Add the coarsely-chopped spinach and the leek cut into rounds. Cover again, and after simmering 15 minutes add the peas, the juice of one pomegranate, and the seed kernels of the other. Cook 10 minutes longer.

4 About 3-4 minutes before the end of cooking time, add about one tablespoon lemon juice and adjust the salt and pepper. In the meantime, wash and dry the leaves of 1 sprig of mint and heat in 3-4 tablespoons oil until limp, adding $1/4$ teaspoon cinnamon and a pinch of pepper. Pour this mixture into the soup, stir, remove from the heat, and ladle into individual serving bowls with the meatballs.

120 g/³/₄ cup rice for soup
1 bunch leafy spinach,
   300 g/³/₄ lb
120 g/¹/₃ lb lentils
100 g/¹/₄ lb shucked peas
1 onion
¹/₂ leek
1 sprig fresh mint
	2 pomegranates
	   (one for juice/one for the
	   seed kernels)
	Ground cinnamon
	Lemon juice
	Salt and pepper
	Olive oil
		For the meatballs:
		300 g/11 oz lean beef
		   (or boned chicken)
		1 egg
		Whole cinnamon, coriander seeds,
		   and peppercorns
		Flour
			Servings: 4
			Preparation time: 25'+2h
			Cooking time: 50'
			Difficulty: ● ● ●
			Flavor: ● ● ●
			Kcal (per serving): 647
			Protein (per serving): 54
			Fat (per serving): 14
			Nutritional value: ● ● ●

SOPA DE LENTEJAS ROJAS

Red Lentil Soup

200 g/7 oz red lentils
250 g/¹⁄₂ lb lamb
   (boned leg or shoulder)
1 onion
2 cloves garlic
Coriander and cumin
1 envelope saffron
Red wine vinegar
Salt and pepper
Olive oil

Servings: 4	
Preparation time: 5'+2h	
Cooking time: 1h	
Difficulty: ● ●	
Flavor: ● ● ●	
Kcal (per serving): 349	
Protein (per serving): 25	
Fat (per serving): 12	
Nutritional value: ● ●	

1 Set the lentils to soak about 2 hours before beginning. Brown the lamb meat slowly (a terracotta pan is best) with 4-5 tablespoons oil. When the meat is uniformly browned, add the sliced onion, the crushed garlic, and salt and pepper.

2 After 4-5 minutes, add the drained lentils and about 1 liter/4 cups water, ¹⁄₂ teaspoon coriander seeds, the same quantity of cumin seeds, and the saffron diluted in 1 tablespoon water. Cover the pan, lower the flame to a minimum, and simmer for about one hour. When tender, remove the meat and cut into cubes.

Add a few drops of vinegar to the soup and add salt and/or pepper if necessary; remove the garlic cloves. Serve in individual bowls with the meat cubes. It is important that the lentils not be overcooked and the soup not watery.

Meat
AND Poultry

*The elegance of the kid and the lamb
in the embrace of intense aromas,
the finesse of rabbit with the fragrant lure of cumin,
the tender delicacy of chicken
enveloped in the golden velvet of the Jerez wines.
And then again, choice pork loin
stewed slowly and ennobled
by the gentle caress of tasty almonds.
Elegant veal and prime beef: in the meat dishes
the ancient art of Andalusian cooking
is revealed to its very best.*

3

700-800 g/1 ½-1 ¾ lbs
boned pork loin,
Málaga muscatel wine
(see note below)
30 g/1 ½ oz shelled and
peeled almonds
30 g/1 ½ oz Málaga raisins
Whole cinnamon
Salt and pepper
Olive oil

Servings:	4
Preparation time:	15'
Cooking time:	1h
Difficulty:	● ●
Flavor:	● ●
Kcal (per serving):	498
Protein (per serving):	40
Fat (per serving):	26
Nutritional value:	● ●

LOMO A LA MALAGUEÑA

Pork Loin Málaga Style

The Málaga muscatel, its high alcohol content (23% on the average), is usually considered a dessert or sipping wine. The color varies from amber to antique gold according to sweetness. As an alternative you may use Marsala, Madeira, or Port wine, on condition it be rather dry.

Soak the raisins in lukewarm water. Rub the loin on all sides with salt and pepper and if necessary tie to hold in shape. Place in an ovenproof/flame-proof pan with 4-5 tablespoons oil and brown uniformly on all sides over a low flame. Remove from the heat, pour in 2 cups wine, crush and add a piece of cinnamon, and place the pan in a preheated 200°C/375-400°F oven. Roast for about 1 hour, basting occasionally with the pan juices (should the meat seem to brown excessively, lower the heat to 180°C/350°F after the first half-hour). In the meantime, blanch the almonds, drain well, and sliver. Toast the slivers in a skillet over high heat (with no fats added) or in the oven where the meat is roasting. When the loin of pork is done, remove from the oven and untie. Serve sliced, moistened with the pan drippings and sprinkled with the squeezed-dry raisins and the toasted almond slivers. Serve the remaining sauce in a gravy boat.

CONEJO AL SALMOREJO

Marinated Rabbit

Rinse and dry the rabbit and cut into 10-12 pieces (excluding the head). Marinate the meat and the liver for 3 hours in ½ cup oil with the peeled and crushed garli[c]... thyme, a pinch of salt, and 3-4 pep[per]... quently so as to uniformly distribut[e]... or drying, transfer the meat and the... with a cover is best) with the straine[d]... id ingredients). Cook the rabbit ove[r]... on all sides, then cover and continu[e]... ble flame for a total of about 45 mi[nutes]... that the meat is not sticking to the... few spoonfuls of hot water or veg[etable]... first: remove it from the pan as s[oon]... transfer to a mortar (or food mill)... bay leaf, and the thyme used in the... seeds, and a teaspoon of ground h[ot]... paste thus obtained, add 2-3 tabl[espoons]... diluted paste into the rabbit pan... the end of cooking time and con[tinue]... constantly, to allow the flavors to... over the pieces immediately before...

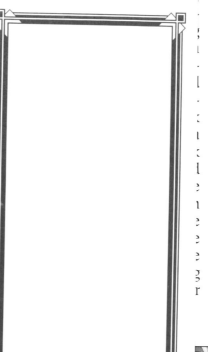

Ingredients
1 rabbit (with liver), ca. 1.3 kg/2 ¾-3 lbs (ready for cooking)
2 heads garlic
Ground hot red pepper (*pimentón*)
Bay leaves and thyme
Cumin seeds
Red wine vinegar
Salt and peppercorns
Olive oil

Servings:	4
Preparation time:	20'+3h
Cooking time:	45'
Difficulty:	● ●
Flavor:	● ● ●
Kcal (per serving):	283
Protein (per serving):	33
Fat (per serving):	16
Nutritional value:	●

CHOTO AJILLO A LA GRANADINA

Kid with Garlic and Spices

1.5 kg/3 1/4-3 1/2 lbs shoulder
  of kid (or lamb), boned
150 g/5-6 oz chicken livers
6 cloves garlic
1 slice bakery bread
  with crust removed
Bay leaves and oregano
1 fresh hot red pepper
Ground hot red pepper
  (*pimentón*)
Red wine vinegar
1/2 liter/2 cups dry white wine
Salt, ground black pepper,
  and peppercorns
Olive oil

Servings: 6	
Preparation time: 25′	
Cooking time: 1h25′	
Difficulty: ● ●	
Flavor: ● ● ●	
Kcal (per serving): 429	
Protein (per serving): 44	
Fat (per serving): 19	
Nutritional value: ● ●	

1 Cut the shoulder meat into uniform, medium-size cubes, and season with a little salt and pepper. Clean the chicken livers (the original recipe calls for the liver of the kid, but this is not always easy to come by today), rinse under cold running water, and dry. Sauté in a skillet with 7-8 tablespoons oil. When done, remove, drain, and reserve.

2 In the oil remaining in the skillet, sauté 4 peeled garlic cloves until golden. Add the finely-crumbled bread and sauté until golden. Remove from the pan with the garlic, drain these ingredients, and reserve. Over low heat, sauté the pieces of kid in the oil remaining in the pan (adding more oil if necessary).

3 Pound in a mortar (or run through a food mill) the livers, the bread, the sautéed garlic cloves, 2 more peeled garlic cloves, 6-7 peppercorns, a good-sized pinch of oregano, the seeded fresh hot red pepper, a teaspoon of ground hot red pepper, and a pinch of salt. Transfer the paste thus obtained to a bowl and dilute with 2-3 tablespoons vinegar and the same amount of wine.

4 Transfer the browned meat to a deep pan with a cover (terracotta is best). Pour the remaining wine into the skillet used for the preceding phases of the recipe and heat slowly to deglaze the pan juices. Add and dissolve the diluted liver-and-pepper paste; pour the sauce over the meat in the deep pan. Add two bay leaves and bring slowly to a boil; cover the pan, lower the flame to minimum, and simmer for at least one hour.

ESTOFADO A LA ANDALUZA

Spicy Beef Stew Andalusia Style

1 kg/2 ¼ lb lean beef
   in a single piece (rump steak
   or other firm cut)
1 sweet pepper
1 ripe tomato
1 onion
2 carrots
3-4 potatoes
1 head of garlic
Bay leaf and parsley
1 small piece whole cinnamon,
   1 clove, and powdered saffron
Jerez *fino* wine (see pp. 92-95)
Salt and peppercorns
Olive oil

Servings: 6-8	
Preparation time: 25′	
Cooking time: 1h30′	
Difficulty: ● ●	
Flavor: ● ● ●	
Kcal (per serving): 469	
Protein (per serving): 36	
Fat (per serving): 12	
Nutritional value: ●	

1 Roast the head of garlic, whole, for about ten minutes under the oven grill, turning occasionally. Separate and peel the cloves. Rinse and trim the pepper, tomato, carrot, and onion.

2 Cut the beef into cubes and brown lightly in a deep pan with a lid (best if terracotta) with 4-5 tablespoons oil, the pepper cut into strips, the tomato in wedges, the sliced onion, and the carrots cut in two lengthwise and then chopped.

3 In a mortar, pound 6 peppercorns with the clove, the roasted garlic, and the small piece of cinnamon to a pasty consistency; add and blend in the saffron. Dilute the paste with a little less than 1 cup hot water and pour it into the pan together with 4-5 tablespoons oil and ½ cup wine; add a bay leaf, one sprig parsley (minced), and a pinch of salt. Cover

the pan and simmer for about 45 minutes, adding hot water if necessary.

4 Add the peeled and sliced potatoes (cut the slices in half if too large). Taste and if necessary adjust the salt. Cover again and simmer for another 20-25 minutes. Serve the *estofado* hot in its terracotta pan.

From Málaga, a typical mosaic made with azulejos.

PATO A LA SEVILLANA

Duck with Citrus Fruit

1 duck, ready for cooking,
 ca. 1.5 kg/3 1/4-3/1/2 lbs
1 onion
1 carrot
1 bitter (Seville) orange,
 or 1/2 sweet orange
 and 1/2 lemon
Brine-packed green olives,
 ca. 180 g (8 oz)
1 bay leaf and parsley
Flour
Vegetable stock
 (made with bouillon cubes),
 ca. 1 liter/4 cups
Jerez *fino* wine,
 ca. 1/2 liter/2 cups
 (see pp. 92-95)
Salt and pepper
Olive oil

Servings: 4-6	
Preparation time: 25'	
Cooking time: 1h40'	
Difficulty: ●●	
Flavor: ●●	
Kcal (per serving): 662	
Protein (per serving): 50	
Fat (per serving): 30	
Nutritional value: ●●●	

1 The duck must be ready for use (plucked, drawn, excess fat and oil sac removed, singed, rinsed, and dried). Cut it into about 12 pieces and brown in a wide, deep pan (terracotta is best, with a lid) with 6 tablespoons of oil and the thinly-sliced onion. When the meat is a deep golden brown all over, remove it from the pan and keep warm. Skim the excess fat from the pan.

2 Add 1 tablespoon flour to the pan drippings and brown, stirring, over moderate heat. Pour in the wine and blend it into the thickened pan drippings, stirring all the time.

3 Replace the pieces of duck in the pan, with the orange (rinsed and cut into wedges but not peeled), a sprig of parsley, a bay leaf, and the peeled, trimmed, and chopped carrot. Season with salt and pepper. Add vegetable stock to almost completely cover the pieces of duck: cover the pan and simmer slowly for about one hour and 20 minutes.
Arrange the pieces on a serving platter and keep warm.

Sevilla, Plaza de España.

4 Strain the pan drippings and return to the pan with the pitted, chopped olives and a few drops vinegar. Heat over a high flame to allow the flavors to blend. Surround the duck with this olive sauce and serve.

POLLO AL JEREZ

Chicken in Jerez Wine Sauce

1 chicken, ready for cooking, ca. 1.2 kg/2 ¾ lbs
3 spring onions
100 g/4 oz cultivated button mushrooms
50 g/2 oz lard, in one piece
Flour
1 bay leaf and parsley
2 dl/¾-1 cup Jerez *fino* wine
Olive oil
Salt and pepper

Servings: 4	
Preparation time: 25'	
Cooking time: 40'	
Difficulty: ● ●	
Flavor: ● ●	
Kcal (per serving): 999	
Protein (per serving): 44	
Fat (per serving): 64	
Nutritional value: ● ● ●	

1 Cut the plucked, drawn, singed, rinsed, and dried chicken into 10-12 pieces and rub each with a little salt and pepper. Sauté the chicken pieces with 5 tablespoons oil to a darkish golden brown; remove to a deep pan and keep warm.

2 Cut the spring onions into rings and dice the lard; stew these ingredients over low heat in the pan drippings. Blend in one tablespoon flour and then add the wine. Cook over high heat for one minute while stirring.

3 Pour this sauce into the pan containing the chicken. Add 1 bay leaf, check and if necessary correct the seasonng, and bring to a boil. Lower the flame, cover the pan, and simmer over very low heat for about ½ hour, adding a little hot water whenever necessary.

4 In the meantime, clean the mushrooms and cut into wedges. Toss in a pan with 3-4 tablespoons olive oil and add to the chicken about 4-5 minutes before the end of cooking time. Arrange the chicken pieces on a serving platter and smother with the mushroom-and-wine sauce; sprinkle with freshly-minced parsley and serve.

As an alternative to the choice Jerez fino, with its fruity flavor and light straw color, you may use any good dry white wine or dry sherry.

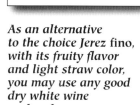

POLLO CON ACEITUNAS

Chicken with Olives

One whole chicken,
  ca. 1.2 kg/2 $\frac{1}{2}$-2 $\frac{3}{4}$ lbs
  (ready for cooking)
24 brine-packed green olives
2 onions
1 clove garlic
1 bay leaf
Jerez *fino* wine
  (see preceding recipe
  and pp. 92-95)
Salt and freshly-ground pepper
Olive oil

Servings: 4	
Preparation time: 20'	
Cooking time: 45'	
Difficulty: ●●	
Flavor: ●●	
Kcal (per serving): 847	
Protein (per serving): 48	
Fat (per serving): 62	
Nutritional value: ●●●	

Prepare the chicken by plucking, drawing, singing, rinsing, and drying. Divide into quarters, plus the spine, and season the pieces with salt and pepper. Peel the onions and chop coarsely with the peeled garlic. Stew the ingredients over low heat (best in a terracotta pan with lid) with 4-5 tablespoons oil. Add the chicken quarters and the back, the olives, and 1 bay leaf. Pour in about 1 cup wine and add enough hot water to almost cover the chicken. Bring to a boil, cover, lower the flame, and simmer for about $\frac{1}{2}$ hour. After this time, remove the chicken quarters from the pan (leaving the back), allow to cool somewhat, and skin and bone. Replace the bones and skin in the pan, cover, and simmer over low heat for another 10 minutes until the cooking liquor is somewhat thickened. Check and if necessary adjust the seasoning. In the meantime, cut the chicken meat into bite-sized pieces and arrange on a serving platter with the olives. Degrease and strain the pan drippings (to eliminate all the solid ingredients, including the skin, bones, and back) and pour over the chicken. Serve hot.

Fish

AND SHELLFISH

The Atlantic and the Mediterranean
vie to supply the boards of Andalusia
with fish of all types. Their freshness is exalted
in refined recipes that unite charm
and flavor in a skillful balance,
even when the combinations
of ingredients are original and unusual.
A perfect accompaniment is offered by
the incomparable white wines of Montilla-Moriles
and of the Condado de Huelva.

4

LABAJÁ DE PESCADO

Fisherman's Stew

1.2 kg/2 ½ lbs assorted fish
(a mix of cod, hake, angler
fish, mullet, devil-fish,
gurnard, tuna, grouper, etc.)
1 onion and 4-5 cloves garlic
1 ripe tomato
Parsley (plus sprigs for garnish)
1 envelope saffron
Jerez *fino* wine
(see pp. 92-95)
2 slices day-old bakery bread
1 lemon (for garnish)
Salt and peppercorns
Olive oil

Servings: 6	
Preparation time: 20'	
Cooking time: 40'	
Difficulty: ● ●	
Flavor: ● ● ●	
Kcal (per serving): 374	
Protein (per serving): 24	
Fat (per serving): 14	
Nutritional value: ● ●	

1 Prepare the fish; scale, gut, cut off tails and fins, rinse well, and cut into pieces. Bring to a boil about 2 liters/2 quarts lightly-salted water with 1 cup wine added, then lower the flame to a minimum so that the liquid barely simmers. Add the fish and cook for 10-12 minutes. Lift out and drain the fish, reserving the cooking liquor.

2 In another pan, cook the peeled and chopped onion and one peeled and crushed clove garlic in 4-5 tablespoons olive oil, until soft. After 3-4 minutes, add the rinsed, seeded, and coarsely chopped tomato and cook over low heat until the tomato is tender. Pour the fish stock into the pan (reserving about 2 ladlesful for later use) and add the crumbled bread.

3 Pound in a mortar (or blend in a food mill) 4-5 peppercorns and one clove garlic; incorporate one envelope of powdered saffron into the paste thus obtained and dissolve in the cooking liquor in the pan with the tomatoes; check and if necessary adjust the salt. Cook for another 5 minutes. Allow the soup to cool a little and serve as a first course, sprinkled with minced parsley.

4 In the meantime, transfer the cooked fish to another pan. In a mortar, pound the remaining garlic cloves with a pinch of salt. Transfer to a bowl and incorporate 1/2 cup oil, then dilute with the reserved fish stock and pour over the fish. Heat without boiling and allow the sauce to thicken slightly. Serve on a platter, garnished with julienned lemon rind and sprigs of parsley.

An appetizing specialty of Algeciras. Like many other recipes from Mediterranean and European maritime tradition, it provides both a first course and an entrée.

ATÚN MECHADO

Larded Tuna

1 tuna steak, 800 g/1 ³/₄ lbs	
70 g/2 ¹/₂ oz lard	
(or unsmoked bacon)	
1 onion	
¹/₂ carrot	
2 cloves garlic	
1 bay leaf	
Parsley	
1 clove	
Flour, about 10 g/1-2 tbsp	
Jerez *fino* wine	
(or other dry white wine,	
see pp. 92-95)	
Salt and pepper	
60 g/2 oz emulsified lard	

Servings: 4	
Preparation time: 20'	
Cooking time: 30'	
Difficulty: ● ●	
Flavor: ● ● ●	
Kcal (per serving): 1076	
Protein (per serving): 43	
Fat (per serving): 89	
Nutritional value: ● ● ●	

C lean and trim the vegetables and herbs in the usual manner. Place the tuna in cold water to "bleed" it; drain and dry. Mince the lard with one clove garlic, the clove, and a pinch of salt. Using a pointed utensil, lard the tuna steak with this mince. Flour lightly on both sides. Melt half the emulsified lard in a skillet and sauté the tuna steak over low heat, turning once, to a golden brown on both sides. Remove from the pan, drain, and keep warm on paper towels. Add the rest of the emulsified lard to the pan and melt; over low heat, cook the sliced onion and remaining garlic clove, the carrot minced with a sprig of parsley, the bay leaf, and a pinch of salt. After about 5 minutes replace the tuna steak in the pan and pour in 1 cup wine plus enough hot water to just cover the fish. Bring to a slow boil and cook for 20 minutes, turning the fish occasionally. Remove the fish to a heated serving platter and cut into strips. Remove the bay leaf from the sauce in the pan and allow to thicken slightly over low heat, blending in 1 tablespoon flour. Pour over the fish and serve.

ATÚN ROJO MARINADO

Marinated Tuna ▶

R inse the tuna and allow it to "bleed." Drain and dry, and cut into paper-thin slices in the manner of carpaccio—or if you prefer, ask your fishmonger to prepare it.
Arrange the tuna slices on a capacious tray, overlapping them as little as possible, and season with salt and pepper. Rinse and trim the spring onions and cut into thin rounds (with some of the green stems); mince the garlic and sprinkle both ingredients over the tuna.
Shake or whisk ¹/₂ cup oil with 3-4 tablespoons vinegar and 1 cup wine. Pour the dressing over the tuna, cover the tray with a sheet of aluminum foil and let stand to marinate for 5-6 hours in a cool place.
Serve the marinated tuna sprinkled with minced parsley.

Instead of slicing the tuna thin like a carpaccio, it may be ground and treated as a tartare or "hamburger": the rest of the preparation is the same. The denomination "generoso" indicates a wine with a high alcohol content, suitable as a dessert or sipping wine, like the Jerez oloroso dulce (but there is also a dry variety) or the veijo muscatel of Málaga; as in other recipes, in this case as well, the Jerez may be substituted with Marsala, Madeira, or Port wine.

Fresh light tuna meat, ca. 600-700 g/1 lb 6 oz-1 ½ lbs	Parsley	Servings: 4	Fat (per serving): 15
4-5 spring onions	White wine vinegar	Preparation time: 10'+6h	Nutritional value: ● ●
3 cloves garlic	Salt and freshly-ground black pepper	Difficulty: ●	
Jerez *generoso* wine (see note on p. 44 and pp. 92-95)	Olive oil	Flavor: ● ● ●	
		Kcal (per serving): 345	
		Protein (per serving): 36	

ANDRAJOS DE JAÉN

Salt Cod and "Scraps"

500 g/1 lb freshened
   and desalted salt cod
   (or cod fillets),
4-5 medium potatoes
2-3 ripe tomatoes
150 g/1 1/4 cups flour
   (plus flour for the board)
4 cloves garlic
Parsley
Ground hot red pepper
   (*pimentón*) and saffron
Fish stock (made with bouillon
   cubes), ca. 1 liter/4 cups
Salt and peppercorns
Olive oil

Servings: 4-6	
Preparation time: 30'+15'	
Cooking time: 30'	
Difficulty: ● ● ●	
Flavor: ● ● ●	
Kcal (per serving): 470	
Protein (per serving): 23	
Fat (per serving): 17	
Nutritional value: ● ●	

1 In a bowl, work enough water into the flour to obtain a firm, uniform dough; shape into a ball and allow to rest for about 15 minutes. Roll out as thinly as possible and cut into irregular strips; flour lightly and reserve.

2 Rinse the tomatoes, seed, and chop. Peel the potatoes and rinse; cut, into cubes. Sauté the potatoes for 3-4 minutes in a deep pan (terracotta is best) with 5 tablespoons oil. Lower the flame and add the tomatoes, while stirring; allow the flavors to blend for 4-5 minutes, adding 1 tablespoon ground hot red pepper. In the meantime, pound the garlic in a mortar (or blend in a food mill) with 2-3 peppercorns, a pinch of saffron, and a sprig of parsley.

3 Cut the salt cod into strips and add to the pan (if cod fillets are used in place of salt cod, add a pinch of salt) with the garlic-and-spice paste. Lay the pasta strips over the top, overlapping the edges.

4 Ladle in enough hot fish stock to just cover and simmer over very low heat (best if the liquid barely bubbles) for about 20 minutes, allowing the liquid to evaporate. Serve the *andrajos* (or "scraps," a specialty of Jaén) hot, sprinkled with minced parsley.

MERLUZA AL ESTILO ANDALUZ

Cod Andalusa Style

700-800 g/1 ¹/₂-1 ³/₄ lbs fresh
   cod fillets
2-3 ripe tomatoes
3 cloves garlic
2 slices bakery bread
Parsley
Shelled hazelnuts
   (about 1 dozen)
Pine nuts
White wine vinegar
Jerez *fino* wine
   (see pp. 92-95)
Salt and pepper, olive oil

Servings: 4	
Preparation time: 15′	
Cooking time: 30′	
Difficulty: ● ●	
Flavor: ● ●	
Kcal (per serving): 556	
Protein (per serving): 36	
Fat (per serving): 27	
Nutritional value: ● ●	

1 Lightly salt the cod fillets and cut into uniform pieces. In a deep pan, sauté the peeled garlic and the crumbled bread in 4-5 tablespoons oil until golden. Remove from the pan with a slotted spoons, drain, place on paper towels, and reserve.

2 In the oil remaining in the pan, sauté the cod fillets briefly until golden (about 1 minute per side). Remove from the pan, drain, and lay on paper towels to dry.

3 Rinse, seed, and finely chop the tomatoes; cook slowly in the oil remaining in the pan, adding more oil if necessary), with a minced sprig of parsley. When the tomatoes are tender (about 10 minutes) add the cod fillets and simmer over very low heat to blend the flavors.

4 While the tomatoes are cooking, pound in a mortar (or blend in a food mill) the sautéed garlic and bread (see step 1), the hazelnuts, and a handful of pine nuts. Dilute the paste thus obtained in a scarce cup wine mixed with 1 tablespoon vinegar. Pour the mixture into the pan containing the fish. Continue cooking for about 5 minutes until the sauce thickens, and serve hot.

CHOCOS CON HABAS

Calamari Squid with Fresh Fava Beans

1 kg/2 ¼ lbs medium-size
  calamari squid
300 g/11 oz fresh fava beans,
  shelled
4 cloves garlic
Parsley (plus parsley sprigs
  for garnish)
Salt and pepper, olive oil

Servings: 6	
Preparation time: 20'	
Cooking time: 30'	
Difficulty: ● ●	
Flavor: ● ●	
Kcal (per serving): 236	
Protein (per serving): 25	
Fat (per serving): 13	
Nutritional value: ●	

Clean the *calamari*: cut off the tentacles at the base and eliminate the cartilage, entrails (including the ink sacs), eyes, and beak. Rinse, dry, and reserve the tentacles; cut the rest into pieces. Peel the garlic and mince finely with the tentacles and a sprig of parsley. In a deep skillet, cook the mince over low heat in 6 tablespoons oil. After 3 minutes, add the squid and cook slowly for 5 minutes more. Add the fava beans, about 2 ladlesful of hot water, and salt and pepper. Cover and simmer for about twenty minutes; remove the cover and continue cooking to evaporate the excess liquid. Serve the dish sprinkled with minced parsley.

This original (and delicious) recipe, from the Atlantic coast of Andalusia, presents an unusual mix of ingredients.

Sevilla: the bridge known as La Barqueta.

PEZ ESPADA A LA MALAGUEÑA

Swordfish with Vegetables

Peel the onion and chop coarsely. Rinse the sweet pepper and the tomatoes, eliminate the seeds and fibrous parts, and cut into small pieces.

Place the vegetables in a large pan with the chopped garlic, a bay leaf, the clove, 4-5 peppercorns, 5 tablespoons of oil, and the lightly-salted swordfish.

Cook over medium heat until the fish is sealed, then add 1 cup wine and bring to a boil. Cover the pan and simmer for just under 20 minutes, until the fish is cooked. Remove the fish from the pan and place it on a serving dish. Sprinkle with chopped parsley and arrange all the cooked vegetables neatly around it before serving.

Swordfish in one slice,
  ca. 900 g/2 lbs
1 onion
4-5 cloves garlic
1 sweet green pepper
2 ripe tomatoes
1 bay leaf
2 cloves
Dry white wine
Parsley
Salt and peppercorns
Olive oil

Servings: 4	
Preparation time: 15′	
Cooking time: 20′	
Difficulty: ●	
Flavor: ●●●	
Kcal (per serving): 430	
Protein (per serving): 49	
Fat (per serving): 17	
Nutritional value: ●	

URTA A LA ROTEÑA

Oven-Roasted Fish with Vegetables

1 Open, gut, skin, and cut the fish into four fillets. Salt lightly and flour on a plate; shake well to eliminate the excess flour. Brown lightly on both sides in a skillet with 5-6 tablespoons oil; remove the fish with a slotted spatula and place on paper towels to dry. Transfer to an ovenproof dish and keep warm.

2 In the oil remaining in the pan, cook the peeled and finely-minced onion and garlic until soft. Then add the rinsed, seeded, and coarsely chopped tomatoes, the green and red peppers (seeded and cut into strips), and 2 bay leaves.

3 Stir while heating to allow the flavors to blend; season with salt and pepper. Pour in 1 cup wine and 2-3 ladlesful of fish stock. Bring slowly to a boil and then turn off the burner.

4 After having removed the bay leaves, turn the contents of the pan into the ovenproof dish containing the fish; sprinkle with breadcrumbs and bake in a preheated 200°C/375-400°F oven for 20 minutes. Serve the fish with roasted potatoes.

1 *urta* (red band bream), ca. 1.2 kg/2 ½ lbs (see note below)
3 ripe tomatoes
1 onion
3 cloves garlic
3 fresh hot green peppers
2 fresh hot red peppers
Jerez *fino* wine (see pp. 92-95)
2 bay leaves
Flour
Pine dry breadcrumbs
Fish stock (made with bouillon cubes)
Roasted potatoes (as a side dish)
Salt and pepper
Olive oil

Servings:	4-6
Preparation time:	20′
Cooking time:	45′
Difficulty:	● ●
Flavor:	● ● ●
Kcal (per serving):	597
Protein (per serving):	38
Fat (per serving):	19
Nutritional value:	● ●

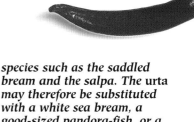

The urta *(Sparus cœruloestictus) is a species of Sparidae that prefers the waters of the beautiful Gulf of Cádiz. The Sparidae (sea breams) are a large and widely-distributed family of fishes including many prized varieties, such as the dentex, the gilthead, and the white bream, and other less "noble"* *species such as the saddled bream and the salpa. The* urta *may therefore be substituted with a white sea bream, a good-sized pandora-fish, or a delicious gilthead. After having been sautéed briefly over high heat in a little hot oil, the potatoes may be roasted in the same pan with the fish.*

DORADA AL JEREZ ▶

Gilthead with Jerez Wine

1 gilthead, ca. 1 kg/2 ¼ lbs
2-3 lemons
Jerez *oloroso* wine
  (see pp. 92-95)
Salt
Olive oil

Servings: 4	
Preparation time: 20'	
Cooking time: 20'	
Difficulty: ●	
Flavor: ●●	
Kcal (per serving): 311	
Protein (per serving): 35	
Fat (per serving): 12	
Nutritional value: ●●	

Prepare the fish for cooking by scaling, clipping the fins, gutting, rinsing inside and out, and drying. Season with salt and pepper in the ventral cavity and introduce a pinch of seasoning into the gill openings. Place the fish in a suitably-sized ovenproof dish. On the upward-facing side, make 3-4 cuts and insert a slice of lemon in each. Sprinkle the fish with lemon juice and a generous dose of olive oil. Pour in ½ cup *oloroso* wine (dry or sweet, according to taste, though we must say that we prefer the sweet version). Bake in a preheated 200°C/375-400°F oven for about 20 minutes, basting the fish from time to time with the pan drippings to keep it from drying out. Arrange on a serving platter; serve a vinaigrette dressing separately.

PESCAÍTO FRITO CON AJO GADITANO

Fried Fish with Piquant Sauce

1 kg/2 ¼ lbs small fish for
  frying (striped bream, cod,
  hake, mullet, anchovy, etc.)
50 g/5-6 tbsp flour
1 lemon (for serving)
Green salad (as a side dish)
Salt, oil for frying

For the ajo:
12 fresh hot green peppers
1 head garlic
2 ripe tomatoes
100 g/¼ lb bakery bread
  with crusts removed
½ lemon
Pimentón fuerte
Salt, olive oil

Servings: 4	
Preparation time: 30'	
Cooking time: 20'	
Difficulty: ●	
Flavor: ●●●	
Kcal (per serving): 655	
Protein (per serving): 33	
Fat (per serving): 42	
Nutritional value: ●●●	

Squeeze the half lemon. Rinse the tomatoes and peppers and remove the stems and seeds. Separate the garlic cloves, peel, and grind in a mortar with the tomatoes and the broken-up peppers, a pinch of salt, and 1 teaspoon *pimentón*. When uniformly mixed, add the crumbled bread and ½ ladleful of boiling water and continue pounding until all the ingredients are perfectly incorporated. Transfer to a bowl and, while mixing, work in enough oil to obtain a sauce consistency; incorporate the lemon juice and allow to stand. Gut, clean, and rinse the fish (if they are very small and very fresh, rinsing is sufficient). Dry and flour. Fry a few at a time in deep hot oil (the anchovies last), remove with a skimmer, drain, and set to dry on paper towels. Sprinkle lightly with salt. Serve the fish hot and crisp with the *ajo* made earlier, lemon wedges, and green salad. This is finger food: each diner will dunk the fried fish in the *ajo*. In addition to the fish suggested above, the *pescaito frito* may include small *calamari* squid, rings of larger squid, and small cuttlefish.

LISA EN AMARILLO

Mullet with Saffron

1 deep-sea mullet,
  ca. 1 kg/2 ¼ lbs
1 onion
2 cloves garlic
1 slice bakery bread
  with crust removed
2 lemons
Parsley
Saffron
Fish stock
  (made with bouillon cubes)
Boiled new potatoes
  with parsley (as a side dish)
Salt
Olive oil

Servings:	4
Preparation time:	15+2h'
Cooking time:	30'
Difficulty:	● ●
Flavor:	● ●
Kcal (per serving):	588
Protein (per serving):	43
Fat (per serving):	27
Nutritional value:	● ●

Gut and scale the fish, trim the fins, and rinse. Cut crosswise into slices about 1.5 cm/½-¾ inch thick (alternatively, skin the fish and fillet). Rub the slices or fillets with salt, sprinkle with the juice of one lemon, and allow to stand for about 2 hours. In the meantime, crumble the bread into a skillet and sauté until golden in 5-6 tablespoons oil; remove and drain. In the oil remaining in the pan, cook the coarsely-chopped onion and garlic until soft. Remove these ingredients and pound in a mortar (or blend in a food mill) with the sautéed bread, a pinch of powdered saffron, and a sprig of parsley, adding enough of the fish stock to obtain a semi-liquid paste. Pour it over the mullet slices arranged in a deep pan and sprinkle with the juice of the other lemon. Place the pan over a low flame and bring to a boil. Cover and simmer for about 10 minutes (adding fish stock as necessary). Serve with boiled potatoes sprinkled with minced parsley or sautéed briefly over high heat in a skillet.

Eggs, Vegetables, and Legumes

The green emporium of Spain and Europe,
Andalusia boasts premier quality vegetables
and excellent legumes:
thus it is only logical that the multifaceted
cuisine of the region
– having found a valid ally in extra virgin olive oil –
vaunts many recipes that make the best of
the freshness and simple goodness
of the native regional products.
And here you'll find some of the most representative.

5

Huevos a la Cordobesa

Eggs Córdoba Style

4 eggs
4 potatoes
1 onion
2 bell peppers
150 g/5-6 oz *chorizo*
  (see pp. 61 and 87)
Salt and pepper
Olive oil

Servings: 4	
Preparation time: 20'	
Cooking time: 30'	
Difficulty: ● ●	
Flavor: ● ●	
Kcal (per serving): 381	
Protein (per serving): 15	
Fat (per serving): 20	
Nutritional value: ● ●	

1 Peel the potatoes, rinse, and cut into thin slices. Peel and likewise slice the onion. Sauté both over low heat in 4-5 tablespoons oil for about 10 minutes. Remove the onions and potatoes with a slotted turner and lay to dry on paper towels.

2 In the meantime trim the peppers, eliminating the stems, seeds, and white fibrous membranes, and cut into strips. Sauté in the oil remaining in the pan (adding more if necessary). Remove with a slotted turner, drain, and lay to dry on paper towels. In the same oil, briefly sauté the sliced *chorizo* until browned on both sides. Cook the eggs in the pan drippings in the following manner. Break an egg and separate the yolk from the white. Let the white fall into the pan and cook over low to moderate heat until nearly firm. Then slip the yolk, seasoned with salt and pepper, onto the center of the white. Cook until the yolk is set but not hardened. Repeat this operation with the other eggs. Arrange the vegetables on a serving platter and top with the eggs; garnish with the fried *chorizo* slices.

HUEVOS REVUELTOS A LA ANDALUZA

Scrambled Eggs Andalusia Style

8 eggs
1 onion
Thyme (for garnish as well)
White wine vinegar
Toasted bread strips
Salt and pepper
Olive oil

Servings: 4	
Preparation time: 10'	
Cooking time: 15'	
Difficulty: ● ●	
Flavor: ● ●	
Kcal (per serving): 481	
Protein (per serving): 25	
Fat (per serving): 30	
Nutritional value: ● ●	

Beat the eggs with a drop of water and a pinch each of salt and pepper, allow the mixture to rest. In the meantime, trim and peel the onion, mince finely, and cook over low heat (best in a terracotta pan) with 4-5 tablespoons oil, a few sprigs of thyme, and a few drops of vinegar, stirring gently. Add the beaten eggs and scramble gently over moderate heat; remove from the heat when the eggs are still creamy at the center of the pan. Garnish with sprigs of thyme and serve as is, with strips of toasted bread.

HUEVOS A LA FLAMENCA

Baked Eggs à la Flamenco

1 Blanch the peas in lightly salted water for 7-8 minutes; drain and reserve. If using the asparagus tips, blanch separately for about 8 minutes, drain, and reserve. Trim the artichokes, eliminating the stems and the toughest outer leaves; blanch for about 10 minutes in lightly salted water. Drain upside-down to spread the leaves.

2 Peel the onion and mince finely with the garlic. Cook until soft in 6 tablespoons oil with the diced ham.

3 Add the rinsed, seeded, and coarsely-chopped tomatoes. Season with salt and pepper and cook over low heat for about 15 minutes.

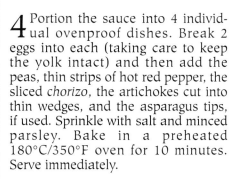

4 Portion the sauce into 4 individual ovenproof dishes. Break 2 eggs into each (taking care to keep the yolk intact) and then add the peas, thin strips of hot red pepper, the sliced *chorizo*, the artichokes cut into thin wedges, and the asparagus tips, if used. Sprinkle with salt and minced parsley. Bake in a preheated 180°C/350°F oven for 10 minutes. Serve immediately.

8 eggs
100 g/¼ lb salt-cured ham (in a single piece)
100 g/¼ lb *chorizo* (see note below and p. 87)
4 ripe tomatoes
100 g/¼ lb shucked peas
2 artichokes
16 asparagus tips (frozen is fine), optional
1 onion
1 clove garlic
1 fresh hot red pepper
Parsley
Salt and pepper
Olive oil

Servings: 4	
Preparation time: 20′	
Cooking time: 40′	
Difficulty: ● ●	
Flavor: ● ● ●	
Kcal (per serving): 637	
Protein (per serving): 35	
Fat (per serving): 48	
Nutritional value: ● ● ●	

Chorizo, *a tasty, highly-spiced fat-and-lean processed pork product (which may or may not contain beef) is similar to the sausage typical of southern Italy. Various types are available on the market, but for cooking we recommend the freshest.*

61

ALCACHOFAS CON HUEVOS ▶

Artichokes and Eggs

4 large artichokes
4 whole eggs and 1 yolk
2 lemons
Ground cumin
Mint and thyme
Salt and pepper
White wine vinegar
Olive oil

Servings: 4	
Preparation time: 20′	
Cooking time: 30′	
Difficulty: ● ● ●	
Flavor: ● ●	
Kcal (per serving): 326	
Protein (per serving): 17	
Fat (per serving): 22	
Nutritional value: ●	

Trim the artichokes, eliminating the stems and the toughest outer leaves; to avoid darkening, plunge into cold water acidulated with the juice of 1 lemon. Boil in lightly salted water, with the addition of 1-2 tablespoons vinegar, for about 20 minutes. Drain and dry upside-down, pressing down slightly to separate the leaves. Beat the egg-yolk with the juice of the other lemon, a pinch of cumin, and a scarce cup of oil to obtain a dense sauce. Let stand.

In the meantime, poach the eggs: break into boiling salted water with a little vinegar added, lower the heat, and cook for about 3 minutes while gently swirling the water so that the white wraps around the egg like a "shirt."

Spread the leaves at the center of each artichoke so as to form a "nest." Place a poached egg on each and top with a teaspoon of sauce. Sprinkle with minced mint leaves and decorate with a few sprigs of thyme. Serve the artichokes at room temperature; invite your guests to help themselves to the remaining sauce.

2 large eggplant
1 onion
1 clove garlic
1 lemon
Parsley, cumin, and oregano
Salt and pepper; coarse salt
 if needed
Olive oil

Servings: 4	
Preparation time: 15′+30′	
Cooking time: 15′	
Difficulty: ●	
Flavor: ● ● ●	
Kcal (per serving): 122	
Protein (per serving): 2	
Fat (per serving): 10	
Nutritional value: ● ●	

BERENJENAS MORISCAS

Eggplant Salad

The excellent Andalusian eggplants are generally very sweet, but should you happen to purchase somewhat pungent ones, slice, lay on a tray, sprinkle with coarse salt, place a weight on top, and let stand for $1/2$ hour until any bitter juice is squeezed out. In the meantime peel and trim the onion and the garlic, and squeeze the lemon. Rinse the eggplant slices, dry, and grill on a rack over coals (or under the over grill), turning once. Peel and dice; place in a bowl. Add the onion minced with the garlic and a sprig of parsley, a pinch of oregano, a small pinch of cumin, and salt and pepper. Dress with olive oil and the lemon juice, mix well, and serve as a side dish with fish dishes.

Espinacas al estilo Cordobés

Spinach Córdoba Style

Fresh spinach,
  ca. 1 kg/2 ¼ lbs
1 onion
2 cloves garlic
Ground cinnamon
Ground hot red pepper
  (*pimentón*)
Red wine vinegar
Salt
Olive oil

Servings: 4	
Preparation time: 15′	
Cooking time: 15′	
Difficulty:	●
Flavor:	●●●
Kcal (per serving):	452
Protein (per serving):	76
Fat (per serving):	11
Nutritional value:	●●●

Pick over the spinach and eliminate the roots and tough stems; wash in several waters until free from sand and soil. Do not dry. Place in a pan, wet, and cook over moderate heat until wilted, without adding water. Drain well and reserve.

Peel the onion and mince finely with the garlic. Cook until soft in a skillet with 3-4 tablespoons oil. Add the coarsely-chopped spinach, one teaspoon *pimentón*, 1 tablespoon vinegar, a pinch of salt, and a pinch of ground cinnamon. Raise the flame and sauté the spinach briefly, while stirring energetically to blend the flavors. Serve hot, preferably as a side dish to rabbit or lamb entrées.

GARBANZOS A LA ANDALUZA

Chickpeas with Peppers

500 g/1 lb chickpeas
250 g/8 oz lard (in one piece)
3 spring onions
3-4 fresh hot green peppers
1 bay leaf
Dry white wine
Salt
Olive oil

Servings: 4	
Preparation time: 15'+4-5h	
Cooking time: 1h	
Difficulty: ● ●	
Flavor: ● ●	
Kcal (per serving): 1159	
Protein (per serving): 28	
Fat (per serving): 79	
Nutritional value: ● ●	

Soak the chickpeas for 4-5 hours before beginning. Drain and place in a deep pan; cover with lightly salted cold water (about 1.5 liters/6 cups). Cover and bring slowly to a boil; simmer for about 45 minutes. At this point, add the spring onions, trimmed and cut in half lengthwise and then into 4 cm/1 ½ inch pieces, the diced lard, 1 cup wine, the bay leaf, and a pinch of salt. Continue cooking, covered, over a low flame until the chickpeas are tender. Check occasionally: it is very important that the legumes remain covered with water for the entire cooking period. In the meantime, rinse and trim the peppers, eliminating stems and seeds, and sauté briefly in 2-3 tablespoons oil. Serve the legumes hot, garnished with the peppers cut into strips.

LIADILLOS SEVILLANOS

Stuffed Cabbage Rolls Seville Style

1 Trim the cabbage, eliminating the toughest outer leaves. Blanch for 2-3 minutes in lightly salted boiling water. Cut out the core and separate the leaves one by one: you will need about a dozen of the largest, whole and tender. Spread the leaves to dry on a cloth, without overlapping.

2 Sauté the ground meat in a skillet with 2-3 tablespoons oil; add the diced bacon and ham. Season with pepper and a little salt (remember that the processed meats are already salty), and grate in a generous dose of nutmeg.

3 Transfer to a bowl and mix in 1 beaten egg, the garlic minced with a sprig of parsley, and the pitted, chopped olives.

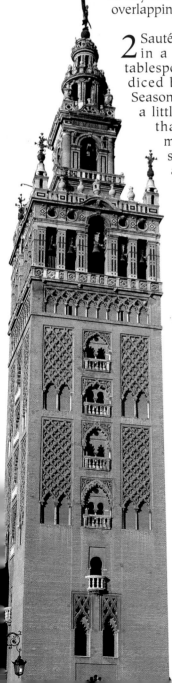

4 Lay a cabbage leaf on a cutting board. Place a little filling at the center and roll up tightly, closing with a toothpick (or kitchen twine). Continue until all the ingredients are used up. Flour the cabbage rolls, dip in beaten egg (until they are well impregnated), roll in the breadcrumbs, and fry in deep hot oil until golden brown. Serve immediately, on a bed of lettuce.

A suggestive view of the Giralda, symbol of the city of Sevilla.

Ingredients
1 head cabbage
150 g/5-6 oz ground lean beef (or chicken)
70 g/3 oz bacon
60 g/2 ½ oz salt-cured ham
3 eggs
1 clove garlic
Black olives, about 20
Nutmeg
20 g/3 tbsp flour
30 g/¼ cup fine dry breadcrumbs
Parsley
Green lettuce (for serving)
Salt and pepper
Oil for frying
Olive oil

Servings: 4-6	
Preparation time: 30'	
Cooking time: 30'	
Difficulty: ● ● ●	
Flavor: ● ●	
Kcal (per serving): 742	
Protein (per serving): 21	
Fat (per serving): 62	
Nutritional value: ● ● ●	

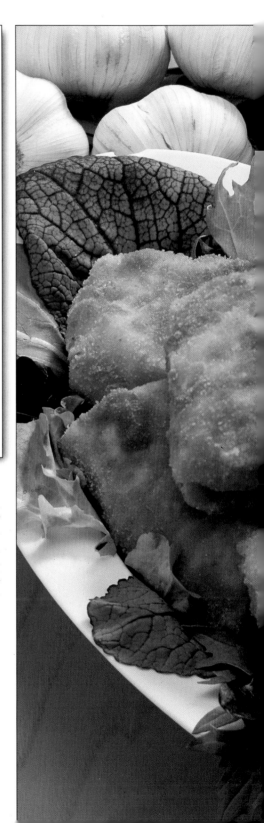

JUDÍAS A LA RONDEÑA

Stewed Beans with Ham

750 g/1 ¾ lbs fresh white
  haricot beans,
  (or 400 g/14 oz if dried)
200 g/½ lb lean salt-cured
  ham, in one slice
2 eggs
4 spring onions
1 ripe tomato
1 clove garlic
Salt and pepper
Olive oil

Servings:	4-6
Preparation time:	15'+6h
Cooking time:	1h
Difficulty:	●●
Flavor:	●●●
Kcal (per serving):	696
Protein (per serving):	37
Fat (per serving):	35
Nutritional value:	●●●

If dry beans are being used, soak in cold water for 6 hours before starting to prepare this dish. Boil the eggs for 7 minutes until hard. Peel the onions and chop them with the garlic, then sauté them (best in a terracotta pan) with 4 tablespoons oil. Rinse the tomato, seed, and cut into pieces; add these to the pan together with the diced ham, the beans, and a pinch of salt and pepper. Pour in hot water until it almost covers the beans, cover the pan, and bring to a boil. Lower the heat and simmer for about 45 minutes. When the beans are cooked *al dente*, boil off any excess liquid, remove from the heat, stir the contents, and garnish with wedges of hard-boiled egg. Serve immediately. These beans are a delicious accompaniment to cold cuts and cheeses. The recipe can also be made using fresh fava beans in season.

Cakes
and Desserts

Lasting Arabian reminiscences,
ancient home-cooking methods,
joyous public events and family celebrations.
Cakes and desserts with the excellence of simplicity
and the richness of genuine ingredients,
the "gusto" of the ideas and substance of tradition.
And to best appreciate such delicacies,
nothing could be better than
one of Andalusia's superb dessert wines.

6

ARROZ CON LECHE

Rice custard

80 g/¹/₂ cup rice
  (suitable for puddings)
6 egg yolks
250 g/1 cup + 2 tbsp sugar
1.3 liters/5 ¹/₄ cups milk
1 vanilla bean
Ground cinnamon
2 lemons
2.5 dl/1 ¹/₄-1 cups whipping
  cream

Servings: 4	
Preparation time: 30'	
Cooking time: 30'	
Difficulty: ● ●	
Kcal (per serving): 894	
Protein (per serving): 31	
Fat (per serving): 46	
Nutritional value: ● ● ●	

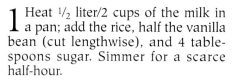

1 Heat ¹/₂ liter/2 cups of the milk in a pan; add the rice, half the vanilla bean (cut lengthwise), and 4 table-spoons sugar. Simmer for a scarce half-hour.

2 In the meantime, place the egg yolks in the top of a double boiler over cold water. Light the burner and beat the yolks over low heat, with the rest of the sugar, until light. When the sugar is completely dissolved, add the rest of the hot (not boiling) milk and the other half of the vanilla bean.

3 Cook the custard over low heat, stirring gently but constantly, until it thickens. Turn off the burner, remove the vanilla bean, and add the cooked rice and a pinch of ground cinnamon. Mix well and allow to cool.

4 Cut pieces of rind from the lemon (in whatever shape you want), taking care to cut the pieces as thick as possible without, however, cutting into the white inner skin. Blanch for 2-3 minutes in boiling water and rinse under cold running water. Whip the cream and fold it into the rice custard. Transfer to a high-sided serving dish. Decorate the surface with the pieces of lemon rind and refrigerate for 3-4 hours. A minute before serving, dust the surface with ground cinnamon.

BORRACHUELOS ▸

Fritters with Jerez Wine

500 g/4 1/4 cups flour
Anise and sesame seeds
Málaga muscatel wine
  (see pp. 92-95)
Jerez *fino* wine (see pp. 92-95)
Juice of 1 bitter orange
100 g/1/3 cup honey
Olive oil

Servings: 4	
Preparation time: 30'+3h	
Cooking time: 30'	
Difficulty: ● ● ●	
Kcal (per serving): 721	
Protein (per serving): 12	
Fat (per serving): 11	
Nutritional value: ● ● ●	

1 Pour a full cup of oil into a pan with 1 tablespoon each of anise and sesame seeds. Heat over a low flame until the oil is hot but not smoking. Turn off the heat and allow to cool completely. Pour the aromatized oil into a bowl (glass is best), and mix in 1 cup each of Málaga muscatel and *fino* wine and the orange juice. A little bit at a time, incorporate the flour with a mixer, taking care to avoid formation of lumps, to obtain a soft, uniform dough. Cover with a cloth and refrigerate for about 2 hours.

2 Divide the dough into balls of such a size as to obtain, after rolling on the board with the palms of the hands, cords about 1 cm/ 1/4-1/3 inch thick and 8 cm/3 inches in length. Moisten and unite the ends to form rounds. Allow to rest for about 1 hour. Fry in deep hot oil, drain, and dry on paper towels. Heat the honey in a saucepan over low heat, stirring constantly so it liquefies without boiling and diluting with a ladleful of warm water. Remove the saucepan from the heat. Immerse the fritters in the honey one at a time, drain well, and arrange on a serving platter.

ROSCOS DE SEMANA SANTA

Holy Week Biscuits

450 g/4 cups flour
4 eggs
100 g/1/2 cup minus 1 tbsp
  sugar
40 g/1 1/2 oz anise seeds
1 clove
Rind of 1/2 lemon
3 g/1 tsp any baking powder
1 dl/1/2-1/3 cup sweet white
  wine
Olive oil

Servings: 6	
Preparation time: 30'+1h	
Cooking time: 20'	
Difficulty: ●	
Kcal (per serving): 832	
Protein (per serving): 17	
Fat (per serving): 20	
Nutritional value: ● ● ●	

In a mortar, grind the anise seeds and the clove to a powder. In a large bowl, mix the flour with the beaten eggs, the sugar, the wine, the baking powder, the finely-grated lemon rind, and the anise and clove powder. Amalgamate well, adding a little lukewarm water if needed, to obtain a uniform, rather soft dough. Allow to rest for 1 hour. Preheat the oven to 220°C/375-400°F.

Place the dough in a pastry bag with a circular tip (1 cm/1/2 inch maximum) and squeeze out into well-distanced forms on a cookie-sheet lined with oiled baking paper. Bake the *roscos* for 20 minutes; remove from the oven and cool. These biscuits are delicious with a glass of the excellent Andalusian desert wines or cordials—even if the combination is not exactly perfect for the last week of Lent.

BRAZO DE GITANO

Custard Sponge Cake

1 To make the *cremadina* (custard) for the filling, slowly heat the milk (do not allow to boil) with the piece of cinnamon and the vanilla bean. In the meantime, beat the egg yolks, sugar, flour, and a pinch of salt with a hand mixer until the mixture is smooth and light.

2 Transfer the egg mixture to the top of a double boiler. Bring the water in the pan underneath to a moderate boil, then add the hot milk to the egg mixture (after having removed the cinnamon and the vanilla bean). While stirring gently, heat the mixture until it just reaches the boiling point. Add two tablespoons hot water and lower the heat to minimum. Cook for 10 minutes, stirring gently all the time. Remove the top pan and mix in the butter cut into small pieces. Allow the *cremadina* to cool; it will thicken as it cools.

3 To make the *brazo* (sponge cake), whip the whites of the eggs until stiff. Blend in the beaten egg yolks one at a time, then the sugar, the flour, and the grated rind of the lemon. Grease a rectangular cake pan (about 30 cm x 35 cm/12 x 14 inches) with butter and line it with greaseproof paper (also buttered). Pour the sponge batter into the pan, smooth the surface, and bake in a preheated 180°C/350°F for about 15 minutes.

4 When done, remove the cake pan from the oven and carefully turn the sponge out onto a sheet of greaseproof paper generously dusted with icing sugar. Spread the *cremadina* in a thick layer over the sponge, reserving a little for decoration. Using the greaseproof paper under the sponge, gently roll up the *brazo* and place on a serving platter with the free end of the sponge underneath and out of sight. Spread the remaining *cremadina* over the roll and dust with icing sugar.

For the custard (cremadina):
2 egg yolks
20 g/2 tbsp finely-granulated
  (castor) sugar
15 g/1 ½ tbsp flour
Whole milk, ca. 2 dl/³⁄₄-1 cup
1 small piece of cinnamon
1 vanilla bean (or a drop of extract)
1 pinch of salt

30 g/1 ½ oz (or 2 tbsp) butter

For the sponge cake (brazo):
6 eggs
80 g/6 tbsp finely-granulated sugar
80 g/7-8 tbsp flour
1 lemon
Icing sugar
40 g/2 oz (or 3 tbsp) butter

Servings: 4	
Preparation time: 35′	
Cooking time: 45′	
Difficulty: ● ● ●	
Kcal (per serving): 294	
Protein (per serving): 6	
Fat (per serving): 14	
Nutritional value: ● ● ●	

DÁTILES FRITOS

Fried Dates

400 g/14 oz dates
Shelled unsalted pistachio nuts
  (as garnish)
Olive oil

Servings: 4
Preparation time: 10'
Cooking time: 5'
Difficulty: ●
Kcal (per serving): 558
Protein (per serving): 3
Fat (per serving): 35
Nutritional value: ● ● ●

Simple as can be and delicious. Rinse and drain the dates and dry well. Heat a full cup of oil in a skillet, over moderate heat, until hot but not smoking. Immerse the dates briefly in the hot oil (10-20 seconds, no more) and then remove with a skimmer. Drain well and place on paper towels to dry. Transfer to a serving platter and serve sprinkled with the finely-chopped pistachios.

TORRIJAS

Fried Bread with Honey

8 slices day-old bakery bread,
  with crusts removed
2 eggs
30 g/2 tbsp light honey
Sweet white muscatel (or similar)
  wine, ca. 2 dl/$^3/_4$ 1 cup
Cinnamon sugar (for decoration)
Oil for frying

U se cookie cutters to cut the bread slices into circles (4-5 cm/1 $^1/_2$-2 inches diameter) and squares (4-5 cm/1 $^1/_2$-2 inches per side). Lay the shapes on a tray and sprinkle with the wine mixed with the honey diluted with 1 tablespoon warm water. Wait about 2 minutes, then turn the shapes over. After another 2 minutes, remove them from the tray, drain without squeezing, and dunk in the beaten egg. Allow the shapes to absorb the egg for a few minutes, then fry in deep hot oil. Remove when golden brown all over, drain, and dry on paper towels. Serve sprinkled with cinnamon sugar or dipped in warm sweetened milk and drizzled with warmed honey.

Servings:	4
Preparation time:	20'
Cooking time:	15'
Difficulty:	● ●
Kcal (per serving):	644
Protein (per serving):	12
Fat (per serving):	30
Nutritional value:	● ● ●

PASTEL DE PIÑONES

Pine Nut Cake

1 Break the eggs into the top of a double boiler over cold water, light the flame, and over low heat mix in the sugar and the flour with a whisk or electric beater. When perfectly amalgamated, spread in a correctly-sized buttered baking pan to a thickness of about 3.5 cm/1-1 ½ inches. Bake in a preheated 180°C/350°F oven for 15 minutes. Remove the cake from the oven and allow to cool before removing from the pan.

2 To make the custard, heat ½ liter/2 cups milk with the vanilla bean, over low heat. In the meantime, beat the eggs with the sugar and then beat the remaining milk into the flour; when smooth, beat into the egg mixture. Transfer to the top of a double boiler over hot water. Pour in the hot milk a little at a time, while stirring, and allow the custard to thicken without ever boiling. Pour into a bowl (glass is best) and continue stirring gently until cool.

3 Split the cake into two layers. Generously sprinkle both halves with Jerez *fino* wine. Spread the custard evenly on the bottom half and cover with the other.

4 Beat the egg-whites until stiff and spread over the surface of the cake. Sprinkle with pine nuts. Bake in a preheated 200°C/375-400°F oven for just the time needed to brown the pine nuts. Remove from the oven and serve sprinkled with confectioners sugar.

200 g/7 oz shelled and peeled pine nuts	20 g/1 ¹/₂ tbsp butter	Servings: 4-6
4 eggs		Preparation time: 30'
120 g/1 cup plus 2 tbsp sugar	*For the custard:*	Cooking time: 50'
150 g/1 ¹/₃ cups flour	4 eggs	Difficulty: ● ● ●
Jerez *oloroso* wine (see pp. 92-95)	6 dl/2 ¹/₃-3 cups milk	Kcal (per serving): 969
2 egg-whites	1 vanilla bean	Protein (per serving): 43
Confectioners sugar	30 g/2 ¹/₂ tbsp sugar	Fat (per serving): 51
	60 g/6 tbsp flour	Nutritional value: ● ● ●

SOPLILLOS GRANADINOS

Granada Meringues

150 g/5-6 oz shelled almonds	
200 g/1 cup minus 1 ½ tbsp sugar	
3 egg-yolks	
1 lemon	
Vanilla extract	
Olive oil	

Servings: 4	
Preparation time: 20'	
Cooking time: 40'	
Difficulty: ● ●	
Kcal (per serving): 626	
Protein (per serving): 18	
Fat (per serving): 39	
Nutritional value: ● ● ●	

B lanch the almonds in boiling unsalted water, peel, and toast in a preheated 220°C/425°F oven. Mince finely in a food mill. Beat the egg-whites until stiff; a little at a time, incorporate the sugar, the juice and grated rind of the lemon, the ground almonds, and a drop of vanilla extract. Place the mixture in a pastry bag with a wide, fluted tip and squeeze out the individual meringues, well-spaced, onto a greased baking sheet. Place in a preheated 140°C/325°F oven for a scarce half-hour, until cooked. Cool and serve.

TYPICAL PRODUCTS AND WINES

7

THE CORNUCOPIA OF SPAIN

As the growing numbers of tourists to Andalusia have discovered, the region enjoys a dry, temperate climate, with hot summers and mild winters. This combination favors fruit and vegetable growing, one of the most important items on the European Union balance sheet. As we will see, the region boasts high-quality dairy products and excellent processed pork specialties, and occupies a preeminent position in the list of contributors to Spain's renowned production in these sectors. Andalusia is an indisputable protagonist in the comestible oil production sector, to which it contributes a wealth of choice extra virgin olive oil. The region also stars in vine-growing and winemaking, giving us the superb, world-famous nectars of Jerez and Málaga and the many other wines of great nobility that have, over time, come to stand alongside them.

Almería: the majestic Alcazaba.

FIELDS AND FLOWERING ORCHARDS

Andalusia, as the Arabs well knew, is Spain's orchard and garden—thanks to the climate, which dispenses abundant harvests over many months. As a matter of fact, the growing period of many varieties extends throughout the entire year, so that export of Andalusian fruits and vegetables accounts for almost a third of Spain's entire production. Fruits of all kinds ripen in the orchards; over time, the traditional varieties—many of which were introduced by the Arabs, to whom also goes the merit for having further developed the plantations introduced in the Roman era—have been flanked by others, which have in part replaced them in the fields. Thus, for example, the succulent *damasquillo* apricots are

less cultivated today than in the past, to the advantage of peaches, nectarines, plums, and citrus fruits. Lemons ripen almost all year round; in competition with the Valencia region, Andalusia also produces great quantities of oranges that brighten the coldest months with their colors and juicy pulp. For the oranges, like for many other crops, Spain must thank the Moors, who originally introduced bitter varieties cultivated for their ornamental value as well as

A picturesque village with its white houses. Andalusia is among the world's largest producers of citrus fruits and strawberries.

for their juice, which is widely used in Moorish cuisine. The sweet orange was brought to Spain from China in the 16th century by the Portuguese, and for this reason is also known as the *china*.

As regards cultivation of sweet oranges— varieties of *Citrus sinensis*, a subtropical species native to China and Indochina— Spain is the world's fourth producer country, after Brazil, the US, and China. But it is the principal exporter, thanks in part to the decisive contribution of Andalusia, where the most important production areas are the Guadalquivir valley between Córdoba and Sevilla, above all near Palma del Rio, and the Andarax valley at the foot of the Sierra Morena. Here, the delicate plants have found an ideal habitat: well-aerated soils with zero salinity and a hot temperate climate with sufficient rainfall, characterized by mild winters (a must for ripening the fruit) and strong insolation in spring and summer, with the many hours of sunlight needed for flowering and fructification. The overwhelming majority of the production is eating oranges: today, the most widely-grown variety is the Navel, with its large, early fruits (75% of Spanish production), followed by the Navelina, Washington, and Thompson varieties and some late cultivars harvested in February and March. Among the bitter oranges, *agrias* or *cachoreñas*, the most famous are the Sevilles: in this case, almost all of the production is transformed into excellent marmalade or squeezed for juice that is used mainly for "cutting" the juice of the sweeter varieties.

Less in quantity, but still very important for the economy of Andalusia, is cultivation of the peach, another fruit native to China, brought to Europe through Persia to Greece and subsequently the rest of the Mediterranean area. *Prunus persica* is a member of the family of the Rosaceae, with a spreading root system that exploits to

the best even the least traces of humidity in the soil; like the orange, it has found an ideal habitat in Andalusia, in the more temperate areas. Thanks to the region's contribution, Spain is Europe's second producer of peaches, topped only by Italy; but differently from the case of Spanish oranges, almost all of the fruit is consumed within the country (70%), only 10% is exported, and the remaining 20% is canned in syrup or used for juice and jam production. The peaches grown in the province of Granada are justly famous, even though the name of the city evokes the pomegranate.

Another Andalusian crop that in fairly recent times has expanded so considerably that it now accounts for 65% of Spanish production (tagged mainly for export) is the strawberry, which has amply repaid the efforts and the investments of many farmers in Andalusia's westernmost province, Huelva. Cultivation of strawberries and giant strawberries is quite widespread in the southern part of the province near the mouths of the Guadalquivir and Guadiana rivers. In this area, the benefits of a subtropical Mediterranean climate (hot-temperate) are associated with those of siliceous soils, rich and well-balanced from the point of view of nutrients, that are well-drained but sufficiently damp thanks to the abundance of water. And of course, Nature's gifts are constantly being flanked by new technologies in agriculture. The production area comprises

three zones: the *comarca litoral* (Moguer, Palos de la Frontera, Lucena del Puerto, and Almonte), the *comarca costa*, east of the first (Lepe, Cartaya, Isla Cristina, and Villablanca), and the *comarca campiña* (Rociana, Bollullos Par del Condado, Palma del Condado, Villalva, Bonares, and Niebla). The most widely-grown variety (98%), which has gradually replaced the European fruits, is the Californian Camarosa: it is large, very early, and brilliant red when ripe with firm, well-colored flesh. Other cultivars include Tudla, Oso Grande (again from California), Cartuno, and Carisma. Strawberries normally ripen in the spring, but in the province of Huelva the mildness of the climate permits almost uninterrupted year-round growing and harvesting. The plants, which require cool nights to best grow and fructify, are often started on the highlands, where the climate is more continental, and then trans-

planted to the shore area where they benefit from the hot climate, strongly influenced by the sea, and the strong insolation (with the province of Almería, the most intense in Spain).

Thanks to the subtropical climate that dominates in many areas, Andalusia also boasts many plantations of exotic crops, especially in the Cueva de Axárquia, the historical cradle of sugar cane. Since the cane was introduced by the Arabs in the 10th century or thereabouts there have also existed transformation facilities for the production of sugar and sugar cane honey (*miel de caña*). This traditional crop does not enjoy the favor it once did: the fertile valleys of the *axarqueño* shore and the terraces that step down to the river valleys now host extensive plantations of avocado, which has adapted perfectly in the region as have other exotic tropical fruits from the New World and the Orient, like mango,

Calle Encarnación in Córdoba.

chirimoya or custard apple, papaya, passion fruit, lychee, and carambola.

Another important activity is production of dried fruit and nuts for consumption both as is and as a fundamental ingredient in many desserts. All the world knows, loves, and uses Málaga raisins, dried on mats in the Andalusian sun; the region also produces and exports great quantities of almonds, walnuts, sugary dried figs, and exquisite prunes. But Andalusia's fruit does not grow exclusively on the shores and in the valleys. There are also the sweet chestnuts of Huelva and the mountainous portion of the province of Granada; most of the production is dried and transformed into the excellent chestnut flour used for preparing traditional desserts or delicate, spreadable chestnut butter. Of note among the derivative products is the honey of the provinces of Córdoba and Jaén, in various essences like orange blossom, eucalyptus, rosemary, and multifloral, and the jams and marmalades of Córdoba, the Guadalhorce valley, and the Serranía de Ronda in the province of Málaga, all made by traditional methods and all without preservatives or coloring agents from cultivated and wild plums, blackberries, and lemons—and, of course, the bitter Seville oranges.

Going on to vegetables, some of the most widely cultivated in Andalusia are asparagus (those of the provinces of Córdoba, the region's great fruit and vegetable emporium, of Granada, and of Jaén are choice quality), broccoli, cabbage, cauliflower, potatoes, and carrots. The Mediterranean province of Almería, the easternmost in the region, is a garden of tomatoes, artichokes, and other vegetables that are harvested almost all year round; most of the production is transformed into excellent *conservas caseras* according to centuries-old traditional methods. The same can be said for the inland province of Jaén, known for its eggplants and its *pimientos de piquillo*, named after their pointed form, moderately hot and the best type for stuffing. Besides these peppers, which ripen in early autumn, Andalusia also

Figs, almonds, walnuts. But not just fruit: Andalusia, Europe's cradle of exotic fruits, is also a cornucopia bursting with delicious vegetables.

produces great quantities of other varieties, large and small. Among those of the first type, of note the large red peppers that are skinned and packed in oil (*pimiento marrón*), and among the second, the extremely hot *guindillas* (liter-

The abundance of excellent vegetables fuels Andalusia's flourishing packing industry.

ally, "little cherries," so-called on account of their form and color—but that's where the resemblance ends!). A compromise, as far as size goes, is represented by the mild *ñoras* or *pimientos choriceros*.

Finally, there are the renowned Andalusian legumes, like the tender chickpeas, the lentils, and the white and red beans.

THE FLAVORS OF TRADITION

Spain goes justly proud of the meats of the lively, lean, black-haired *cerdo ibérico* (Black Iberian pig), used to make a rich variety of products. Andalusia, in particular, boasts fine salamis and excellent sausages redolent of garlic, and reserves a PDO (Protected Designation of Origin) mark for the choice-quality cured ham that under the name of "Jamón de Huelva" has won worldwide fame for one of its most beautiful and evocative provinces, stretching from the eastern tip of the stupendous Sierra Morena to the Portuguese border. In the woods of scrub, cork, and holm oak that mantle the mountains uniting Andalusia and Extremadura, in an environment unique in the world for its naturalistic and landscape value, the prized *cerdo ibérico* is reared in the

wild state. The meat is hand-processed only in the same area; the ability of the mountain pork butchers to treat hams and pork shoulders with traditional methods that guarantee unmistakable aromas, textures, and flavors has been known and appreciated for centuries. The area covered by the PDO is limited to 31 municipalities in the Sierra de Huelva; of particular importance are Almonaster la Real, Aracena, Aroche, Corteconcepción, Cortegana, Cumbres Mayores, Jabugo, and Santa Olalla del Cala.

Huelva hams are recognizable at first sight, with their slim, never-too-rounded silhouette, their markedly triangular form, and the slender bone with the hoof usually still attached; the inner face is covered with the characteristic whitish patina of microflora typical of slow, natural aging. The meat, lean, aromatic, and finely-grained with thin veins of fat, is rose-colored shading to deep red according to the duration of the aging process, which lasts from a minimum of seven months to a few years. Although of slightly lesser quality, the PDO ham-cured shoulder presents analogous characteristics. The Huelva hams and shoulders all carry the specifications listed below on a band required by law, with marks of different colors identifying the conditions in which the pigs were reared. These are *de bellota* (literally, "of acorns"), by far the choicest, indicating *cerdo ibérico* animals raised in the wild on a diet made up exclusively with acorns and other natural forest foods (red band and seal); *de recebo*, indicating pigs raised in the wild whose diet of acorns and other natural foods is integrated with authorized feeds (blue mark and seal); and *de pienso* (literally, "of feed"), indicating pigs raised in the semi-wild state on authorized feeds (yellow band and seal). Huelva ham is best eaten thinly sliced and makes a satisfying meal in itself. Other choice Andalusian hams are those produced from the *cerdo ibérico* in the Los Pedroches valley, near Córdoba, and those of the province of Granada.

Among the Andalusian localities famous for their sausages (besides, naturally, the Huelva area), are the province of Cádiz, where they are often smoke-cured, and the provinces of Córdoba, Granada, and Jaén. The *chorizo* is a semihard sausage of lean and fatty ground pork flavored with ground hot red pepper, garlic, and black pepper. It is eaten at virtually all stages of aging; if fresh, it is best cooked. Of great renown are the bright red, U-shaped *chorizo* of Jabugo, produced in the heart of the Huelva PDO ham production area, and the small, dark red *chorizos de Málaga*.

The *longaniza* is a hard or semihard sausage of lean and fatty ground pork, and as the name suggests it is long and thin, sometimes curved into a "U". It is aged for a medium period, is sometimes

Besides the famous cured ham and pork shoulder (next page, bottom), Andalusia produces a wide variety of sausages.

hot-spicy, and is eaten uncooked. Pig's blood is the main ingredient in the *morcilla* (blood sausage); it is often flavored with spices (anise, cinnamon, and cloves) and sometimes includes rice and pine nuts; it is eaten cooked, and is the basic ingredient in many typical recipes with vegetables or legumes. Among the best known types are the *morcilla granadina de cebolla*, a smooth, plump, purple-black sausage, flavored—as the name suggests—with finely-minced onion, the likewise very dark-colored *morcilla serrana* of Jabugo, and the *morcilla* of Córdoba, which includes rice or onion.

GIFTS OF THE PASTURES

The geographical and historical peculiarities of Andalusia, the climate, and the configuration of the terrain have always worked to strongly favor sheep- and goat-herding over cattle-raising.

Consequently, the milk of the former animals is that most commonly used in the cheese-making industry: the great majority of production, which is copious and very high-quality, is sold on the domestic market. Describing the areas of Andalusia most renowned for their production of fine cheese, which often correspond to the areas mentioned in regard of processed pork products and oil, is tantamount to visiting some of the region's most beautiful landscapes. We will begin with the Las Alpujarras hills, between the Contraviesa ridge and the Sierra Nevada, dense with cultivated fields and orchards and extensive pastures for the autochthonous white goats, renowned for their fatty, dense, aromatic milk, raised in the half-wild state, and accustomed to changing pastures according to the season.

The fresh and aged cheeses of Alpujarras, made with unpasteurized goat's milk mainly in winter and early spring, are mild but distinctive, with a definitely milky, slightly salty flavor with a light spicy note and an aroma of nuts and hay. The pressed cheese is semifirm, marble-white in color with tiny holes and a light, buttery texture. The forms, weighing 1.2 kg/2 ^{1}/$_2$-2 ^{3}/$_4$ lbs on the average, have a natural straw-colored, brushed or oiled rind impressed with the typical wheat head pattern on both sides and textured by the marks left by the esparto grass baskets used for their making.

The province of Cádiz produces excellent cheeses in the mountainous eastern area where the Sierra de Grazalema rises, and in particular in the territories of the municipalities of Villaluenga del Rosario, Benaolcaz, and Grazalema. At the border with the province of Málaga, the area is a peculiar ecosystem: cultivated land is a rarity and much space is reserved for high pastures, where breeding, herding, and traditional cheese-making activities have been conducted for centuries. The sheep's milk cheeses of Grazalema, very similar to the *manchego*, the well-known and appetizing Spanish pecorino, are eaten fresh, ripened, and aged. Their pleasing flavor becomes more pungent and salty as they age; the rind is hard and the cheese light-colored with close-set holes. In other mountain areas of Cádiz we find choice qualities of snow-white fresh goat's-milk cheese, with their sharp but pleasing flavor; they are pierced by many small holes and are ideal with the Jerez wines.

To the west, at the western tip of the Sierra Morena, is the Sierra de Huelva or de Aracena, a series of undulating highlands at an average altitude of 600 meters above sea level, culminating in the Cerro del Castaño (962 m). The climate here is temperate; in large part, the landscape is dominated by woods of Mediterranean essences in which the scrub oak stands alongside the cork oak and where the *cerdo ibérico* feeds on acorns. For its environmental and landscape value and the variety of its flora and fauna (including the black vulture), the area has been awarded the status of Natural Park. Within the park territory are villages of great historical and artistic value, where the ancient religious, folk, and materic traditions are perpetuated; one of these, and not the least important, is cheese making. The aged cheese of Aracena is produced from the unpasteurized milk of the autochthonous Serrana goat, known for giving small quantities of very high quality milk. This semifirm cheese has a distinctive flavor that goes well with the *fino* and *amontadillo* types of Jerez wine; the flavor is more delicate when the cheese is made during cold and humid periods.

The forms, weighing 1 kg/2 ¼ lbs on the average, are cylindrical and slightly depressed but may also be low and flattened (the so-called *torta*). The rind is wrinkled and "sticky," and blue-green in color with brown spots due to the bacterial flora that covers it. The rind of the variety called *queso sudado* is covered with efflorescences and spontaneous molds that vary in color according to the climatic conditions and season but generally tend to tones of orange. This cheese is made by hand—no two forms are alike—and ripened at ambient temperature.

Among the other renowned cheese production areas are the territory of Pozo Alcón, in the province of Jaén at the edge of the Sierra de Cazorla Natural Park, and the Los Pedroches valley, in the northeastern part of the province of Córdoba, with La Serena and the Alcudia valley. The cheeses of the Sierra de Cazorla, put on the table after a brief period (3 to 5 months) of ripening at controlled temperature (10-14°C/50-57°F) and high humidity, are made from pasteurized goat's milk coagulated at 30-32°C/86-90°F. The white, semifirm cheese, with few or no holes, is buttery in texture and strongly flavored with mild overtones. The forms, generally weighing a little less than 1 kg/2 ¼ lbs, are cylindrical with flat faces (wheels); the wrapping of parkland aromatic herbs (mainly thyme and rosemary) transmits its subtle and balanced aroma to the cheese,

which is excellent with dried fruit and nuts. The salty type is flavored by immersion in brine. The traditional semi-ripened cheeses of Los Pedroches are instead produced, in the winter and spring, from the unpasteurized milk of sheep, mainly the Merinos breed. The cheese is strongly flavored and hard, with a creamy texture. The cylindrical wheels, with flat faces, rounded edges, and wrinkled sides, weighing 1.7 kg/3 ¾ lbs on the average, are ripened for 2 to 4 months. The straw-colored rind is firm, shiny, and slightly oily; the cheese is marble-white in color and compact in texture, with very fine, irregularly distributed holes. If these cheeses are aged, the color shifts to yellowish ivory, the aroma intensifies, and the flavor becomes saltier and sharper. They are also often preserved in oil in clay pots, as are the snow-white goat's-milk cheeses of the province of Málaga, and, like the latter, they carry the print of the reed baskets in which they ripen.

Almería: a characteristic home carved in the tufaceous rock in the Chanco district. Opposite, top, the Patio Judería.

GREEN GOLD

The olive tree has always been a dominating element of the Andalusian landscape, especially in the provinces of Córdoba, Granada, and Jaén; the *hojiblanca* variety of olive prospers around Antequera and Cueva de Axárquia in the territory of Málaga. In Andalusia, olives grow even at altitudes that would be prohibitive in other Mediterranean countries, thanks to the favorable climate, to

which we also owe the mildness of the well-known table olives with their thin skins and delicate pulp, like the famous *manzanillas* of Sevilla.

No wonder, then, that olive oil is one of the principal alimentary and economic resources of the region. Its success is assured by the perpetuation of ancient traditions but also to the Andalusian producers' talent for keeping in step with the times by promoting a never-ending process of perfecting production techniques that has raised their oil to levels of excellence in the world panorama. Andalusia holds seven of Spain's thirteen *denominacions de origen* (designations of origin, or D.O.) quality labels for olive oil: Baena, Montes de Granada, Priego de Córdoba, Sierra de Cádiz, Sierra de Cazorla, Sierra de Segura, and Sierra Mágina. These are very high-quality extra virgin olive oils, from olive groves listed in special registers and characterized by controlled planting densities; the oil is cold-pressed only from the prescribed varieties of olives and bottled in the same D.O. production zones.

Baena The zone of production encompasses the territories of the municipalities of Baena, Castro del Río, Doña Mencía, Luque, Nueva Carteya, and Zuheros in the southwestern part of the province of Córdoba. The area's rivers are the Guadajoz, the Marbella, and the Guadalmoral; the hill-country soil is prevalently calcareous. In the area, with its temperate continental climate with dry, hot summers and limited precipitation, the olive has been cultivated since Roman times. The Arabs gave a considerable boost to olive cultivation: in the 12th century the olive was the predominant crop, at the same level with grains. The oil, of very high quality, has a fruity, aromatic bouquet; the color varies from green to yellow according to the ripeness of the olives. The oil is pressed mainly from olives of the Picuda variety, with other types in lesser percentages (Lechin, Chorúa, Pajarero, Hojiblanca, and Picual). The olives may be harvested manually by the methods called *ordeño* (hand-picked from the trees) and *vareo* (consisting in beating the branches with sticks), or they may be made to fall by the vibration transmitted to the trunk by special machinery.

Montes de Granada This extensive production zone, bordered to the north by the provinces of Jaén and Córdoba and to the south by the fertile Granada valley, embraces the territories of the municipalities of Alamedilla, Albolote, Alfacar, Alicún de Ortega, Atarfe, Benalúa de las Villas, Calicasas, Campotéjar, Cogollos Vega, Colomera, Darro, Dehesas de Guadix, Deifontes, Diezma, Fonelas, Gobernador, Guadahortuna, Güevéjar, Huélago, Iznalloz, La Peza, Moclin, Montejícar, Montillana, Morelábor, Nívar, Pedro Martínez, Piñar, Torre-Cardela, and Villanueva de Las Torres. The area is characterized by high altitudes and a Mediterranean-continental climate with

long, cold winters with frequent snowfalls (a great aid in the fight against parasites) and long, hot, dry summers; the oils produced here are highly aromatic and tend to be somewhat bitter in taste. Olive cultivation has been carried on in the area since ancient times and has never suffered significant interruptions; the quality of the oils has always remained high, thanks in part to the perpetuation of the traditional growing and processing methods. The D.O. applies to two types of oil: one intensely fruity, with a bouquet recalling the green olive, greenish in color, and pleasantly, slightly bitter in flavor, and the other *suave:* fruity, with a lighter bouquet, tending to yellow in color, and with a more delicate flavor. The oil is pressed mainly (80%) from olives of the Picual and Marteña varieties, which are hardy and resistant to the winter cold, with 15% of the Lucio and Loaime (the name is of Arab origin) varieties, autochthons of the province of Granada that are both drought- and frost-resistant, and lesser percentages of the Negrillo de Iznalloz, Escarabajuelo, Gordal de Granada, and Hojiblanca cultivars.

Priego de Córdoba The zone of production, situated in the southeastern part of the province of Córdoba in the heart of the Sierras Subbéticas Natural Park, borders the provinces of Jaén and Granada and embraces the territories of the municipalities of Priego de Córdoba, Almedinilla, Carcabuey, and Fuente-Tojar. The area's rivers are the

Bottles of premium-quality Andalusian extra virgin olive oil.
Below, Málaga: the port and the Paseo del Parque.

Salado, the Caicena, and the Zagrilla; the climate is distinguished by heavy precipitation and a broad temperature range. Here too, olive cultivation began in Roman times and has continued without interruption down to the present day as one of the principal economic resources and the area's most important crop. The oil, of exceptional quality, with a fruity bouquet and a mild flavor with hints of the spicy and the bitter, is pressed mainly from the frost-resistant Picuda variety, and in lesser percentages from the Hojiblanca and Picual olives, which ripen at altitudes above 700 meters on heavily-eroded, rocky, prevalently calcareous soils with inclusions of clay and sandstone.

Sierra de Cádiz The zone of production, in an agricultural area where stockbreeding is also carried on, is irrigated by the Guadalete and Guadalporcún rivers. Framed by the Algodonales and Líjar mountains and bordered on the southwest by the Sierra de Grazalema, it comprises the territories of municipalities in the provinces of Cádiz (Alcalá del Valle, Algodonales, Olvera, Setenil de las Bodegas, Torre-Alháquime, and Zahara de la Sierra) and of Sevilla (Coripe and Pruna), set in an exceptional landscape. The calcareous soils and the precipitation, the heaviest in all of Spain, are favorable to the olive plantations that dominate in the area. The clear oils of this D.O. have an intense, medium-fruity bouquet of green or ripe olives with hints of woodland fruits and fragrances, and a balanced, slightly bitter/spicy flavor. They are pressed mainly from olives of early, vigorous, high-yield, Lechín variety (a plant that is widely distributed throughout the Mediterranean basin, and especially in Italy), which thrives on highly calcareous soils, with other varieties in lesser percentages: Manzanilla, Verdial, Hojiblanca, Picual, Alameña, and Arbequina, in decreasing order of importance.

Sierra de Cazorla The production zone, bordering on the natural park of the same name in the southeastern part of the province of Jaén (also mentioned in the section on cheeses) is delimited to the northeast by the Sierra de Segura, to the north by the upper Guadalquivir valley, to the west by the Baza and Huescar tablelands in the province of Granada, and to the west by the mountains of Jaén. Oil has been produced here since antiquity; production was consolidated in the Roman era and even more so during Arab domination; today, the olive is the principal cultivation in the area. Of great landscape value, the zone of production includes territories in the municipalities of Cazorla, Chilluévar, Hinojares, Huesa, La Iruela, Peal de Becerro, Pozo Alcón, Quesada, and Santo Tomé that produce oils with often widely-differing characteristics, since the groves are situated at varying altitudes. Common characteristics, besides of course the excellent quality (deriving in part from the fact that all the olives are cold-pressed), are a slightly bitter flavor, extremely low acidity, and the high stability that determines frequent use of these oils for cutting less balanced products. The great majority of the olives are of the Picual variety (so-called after its slightly pointed form), followed at a distance by the choice Royal cultivar, which is grown mainly in the territories of Cazorla, La Iruela, and Quesada.

Sierra de Segura The zone of production, for the most part mountainous and, traditionally, with an identity all its own from both the landscape and cultural points of view (and in the past also recognized as a separate administrative district), is situated in the northeastern part of the province of Jaén, and in large part is coincident with the natural park of the same name. The altitude in the area varies, although it is prevalently high: the highest portion, a mountainous massif characterized by a rich variety of flora and fauna, with vast areas of Mediterranean woodlands and the springs of the Guadalquivir, the Segura, and the Guadalimar rivers, contrasts with the lower-altitude area, where olive groves cover the steep slopes up to the edges of the woods. The olive has always

been an important resource in this damp area that embraces the territories of the municipalities of Beas de Segura, Benatae, Chiclana de Segura, Génave, Hornos de Segura, La Puerta de Segura, Orcera, Puente de Génave, Santiago de la Espada-Pontones, Segura de la Sierra, Siles, Torres de Albánchez, and Villarrodrigo. By far the most common variety of olive is the hardy Picual, resistant to both parasites and climatic adversity; it is followed by small percentages Verdala, Royal, and Manzanillo de Jaén olives. The oils of this D.O., of premium quality with very low acidity, are fruity and well-balanced. The zone also produces choice single-variety oils and oils from organically-grown olives.

Sierra Mágina This beautiful production zone surrounds the massif for which it is named, in an area with peaks exceeding 2000 meters (culminating in the Pico Mágina at 2167 m) and of such naturalistic and landscape value as to have been designated a natural park, at the center of the province of Jaén and extending across the Jandulilla, Guadiana Menor, and Guadalquivir valleys to the borders of the administrative district of Granada. For the most part, the climate is Mediterranean-continental, with pleasant springs and autumns, hot summers, and, due in part to the high altitude, snowy winters. The D.O. covers the production of the territories of the municipalities of Albánchez de Úbeda, Bedmar-Garcíez, Bélmez de la Moraleda, Cabra del Santo Cristo, Cambil-Arbuniel, Campillo de Arenas, Cárcheles (Cárchel y Carchelejo), Huelma-Solera, Jimena, Jódar, La Guardia de Jaén, Larva, Mancha Real, Pegalajar, and Torres. In this case as well, the great majority of the olives are of the Picual variety (also the most widely-distributed in the province), which gives us slightly bitter, fruity, stable oils with very low acidity, accompanied in lesser percentages by the fleshy Manzanillo de Jaén.

TREASURES FROM THE WINE CELLAR

Like the olive tree, the vine is a dominating presence in the Andalusian landscape, an essential element, a part of it since time immemorial. It is said that vine-growing and wine-making were introduced at the times of the Phoenicians and Greek colonization; it is certain that during the Roman era the activities were encouraged and became so ingrained to the land and the people that they could not be completely eradicated by the Arab kingdoms, whose policies with regard to alcoholic beverages were notoriously hostile. The Islamic conquerors, forced to drop the prohibition, restricted their actions to imposing fines (the *garima*) and later on only taxes that plumped up the treasury. Following the Reconquista, one of the principal concerns of the Spanish rulers was to return the vine-growing and wine-making activity to its former splendor by providing all possible incentives for these activities. And it wasn't long before the quality of the Andalusian wines was known well beyond the borders of Spain.

Like in the case of other crops, the Andalusian climate, which with its hot, dry summers raises the sugar content of the grapes, combines with the fertility of the soils to produce abundant harvests. And once again, nature's benevolence has been aided by man's knowledge and skill in developing highly-refined vinification and aging techniques—first and foremost, the famous solera method—that guarantee the unchanging quality of the region's world-famous wines. Andalusia holds only four of Spain's more than fifty *denominacions de origen* (designations of origin, or D.O.)—Condado de Huelva, Jerez ("sherry" in the English-speaking world), Málaga, and Montilla-Moriles—but their fame and prestige are more than sufficient to accord the region a position of excellence as a producer of superb wines, the best known being the dessert and sipping (or "conversation" and "meditation") wines.

Condado de Huelva The designation

Bottles with the famous names of renowned Andalusian wine cellars, where the precious nectars of Jerez e Málaga are aged.

is inspired by the historical Condado de Niebla; the zone of production is characterized by a temperate climate influenced by the Atlantic currents, with humid winds from the west and southwest that bring considerable precipitation, but also by the strong insolation. The vineyards rise on permeable and sufficiently fertile soils in the territories of the municipalities of Niebla, Bollulos del Condado, Paterna, Bonares, Chucena, Hinojos, Rociana del Condado, Manzanilla, and Palos de la Frontera, plus those of another eight of the area's towns. Production includes dry, medium dry, medium sweet, and sweet white wines pressed from grapes of the Zalema, Moscatel, Garrido Fino, and Listán (Palomino) varieties. The aromatic young table wines are delicate, smooth, and fruity and perfect with shellfish and fish dishes. Since they also support aging, the Condado wines are also partner well with "white" meats and the excellent Jabugo hams. The young wines are flanked by the *generosos*, which must age in oaken casks for at least 2 years or be matured by the solera blending method. The alcohol level of the young wines varies between 9.5 and 13.5 percent by volume and that of the *blanco de mesa* in particular between 11 and 14 percent. Among the *generosos*, the *Condado pálido* (which may also be produced from organically-grown grapes) weighs in at 15-17%, while the *Condado dulce* reaches 22% and the mahogany-hued *Condado viejo*, 23%. In absolute terms, the best vintages are 1993 and 1999.

Jerez The Jerez wines are probably the most famous of all the Spanish D.O. nectars: also known by the English term "sherry," they come from the town of the same name, Jerez de la Frontera, and its territory. The celebrity of these wines, of very ancient tradition, is such as to have made them models that throughout Andalusia that have influenced the types of wine produced under the other designations. The vineyards stand on white, undulating, calcareous terrains, the famous spongy, deep *al-barizas* that hold water in quantity and at the same time, with their light color, augment the effects of the strong insolation. Rainfall in the hot southern climate of the area, which is strongly influenced by the Atlantic, is not particularly heavy. The zone of production, in the province of Cádiz and watered by the Guadalquivir and Guadalete rivers, extends over the territories of the municipalities of Jerez de la Frontera, Puerto de Santa María, Puerto Real, Chiclana, Chipiona, Rota, Trebujena, and Sanlúcar de Barrameda. The grapes come from vines of the Palomino de Jerez and Palomino Fino (95%), Pedro Ximénez, and Moscatel varieties. Vinification takes place in oaken casks of modest capacity in the cellars in Jerez de la Frontera, Puerto de Santa María, or Sanlúcar de Barrameda, by traditional aging methods, most commonly by the age-old solera system. This traditional system consists of fractional blending of wines of different vintages: about one-third of the wine from one of the oldest casks is withdrawn for bottling and replaced with wine one year younger; this cask is topped up with that from another, again a year younger, and so on.

The designation groups dry aperitif wines and sweet dessert wines that must be aged at least three years before they can be put on the market. The alcohol-by-volume range is very high (between 15 and 20 percent) and there are many different types. Within the dry range, excellent as aperitifs and with olives, crustaceans, mollusks, or light first courses, we have the light straw color *finos* (which may also be produced from organically-grown grapes), with their slightly nutty, dry and delicate flavor and bouquet, containing 15.5-18% alcohol; the

light yellow *manzanilla* (15-19% alcohol), with a delicate and slightly bitter flavor and bouquet, which is vinified only in the Sanlúcar de Barrameda ocean-facing territory and therefore holds its own specification within the designation (as it ages, this wine takes on a topaz hue and a much more mature flavor); and the amber-colored *amontillado*, with its intense and pungent bouquet and containing as much as 18% alcohol.

The range of medium dry and medium sweet wines includes the full-bodied, dry or slightly sweet *olorosos*, with less intense but more persistent bouquets than the *finos*, a deep gold color that tends to darken with aging, and 18-20% alcohol by volume; the *raya*, similar to the *oloroso* but darker in color, containing 17-22% alcohol; and the velvety, antique-gold color *palo cortado*, similar to the *oloroso* to the palate and to the *amontillado* to the nose.

The smooth, mahogany-colored sweet wines are nectars to accompany dessert "conversation", and "meditation". The types are the velvety Pedro Ximénez and the Moscatel, vinified from grapes of the same names ripened to complete maturity in the sunny vineyards. Cream sherry, with characteristics like those of the *oloroso*, is similar, as far as flavor and bouquet go, to the Pedro Ximénez. The sweet wines generally have about 22% alcohol by volume, but the *dulce blanco* type may contain as little as 11%.

Málaga The superb wines of this D.O. are vinified from Pedro Ximénez grapes with lesser percentages of Moscatel (also excellent table grapes), which are nevertheless essential to the sweet types. The grapes are harvested in an area comprising all the towns in the province of Málaga, from the shore to Antequera, where we find prevalently siliceous soils and a climate that is continental in the north, with short winters and summers,

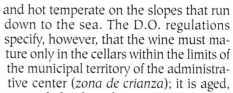

Andalusian wines are matured by the solera *system of fractional blending of wines of different vintages.*

and hot temperate on the slopes that run down to the sea. The D.O. regulations specify, however, that the wine must mature only in the cellars within the limits of the municipal territory of the administrative center (*zona de crianza*); it is aged, mostly by the solera system, in oaken casks. The Málaga wines, high in sugar and alcohol (15-23%), are aristocratic nectars for accompanying desserts, fruit, and fresh cheeses, and of course excellent sipping wines for conversation and meditation. The color varies from a rich burnished gold to very deep amber. The finest of the Málaga wines is probably the *Lágrima* type, vinified from must obtained exclusively by manual methods with no mechanical pressure whatsoever. Recently, besides the historical wines based on white grapes, Málaga's production includes the wines of a new designation, Sierra de Málaga, which also contemplates red wines.

There are many types of Málaga wines. According to composition, the D.O. admits *de licor, dulces naturales*, and *naturalmente dulces* wines. The *vinos de licor* are fortified with neutral spirit and sometimes concentrated must and dry wines from Doradilla, Lairen (or Airén), and Romé grapes, for a maximum tenor of 30% alcohol. The *dulces naturales* and *naturalmente dulces* wines are vinified mainly from sweet grape musts in a percentage of 50% or more. A further classification defines those wines with a sugar content of more than 45 grams/liter as "sweet", between 12 and 45 g/l as "medium sweet", between 4 and 12 g/l as "medium dry" and less than 4 g/l as "dry". By aging period, the types are Málaga (6-24 months), Málaga Noble (2-3 years, Málaga Añejo (3-5 years), and Málaga Trasañejo (more than 5 years). The name Málaga Pálido designates wines to which no concentrated must (*arrope*) has been added and which are marketed without being aged. The D.O. regulations also state that the grapevine names Pero Ximén (or Pedro Ximénez) and Moscatel may be used on the label only when they contribute by at least 85% to the wine.

The *vinos de licor* vinified without addition of *arrope* are the *pálidos* (*Dry Pale* or *Pale Dry*) types, with a sugar content not exceeding 45 g/l, and the *Pale Cream*, also a *dulce natural* or

naturalmente dulce type, with a sugar content of more than 45 g/l. The aged types include the *Dorado* or *Golden* (also *dulce natural* or *naturalmente dulce*) and the amber-hued *Pajarete* (also *dulce natural*) with a sugar content between 45 and 140 g/l. The *Dulce Crema* or *Cream* type (also *dulce natural*) has a 100-140 g/l sugar content and its amber color may be quite intense; the color of the *Sweet* type (also *dulce natural*), with more than 140 g/l sugar content, ranges from amber to "black." The styles of the aged *vinos de licor* with *arrope* added are the *Rojo dorado* or *Tawny* (addition not exceeding 5%), *Oscuro* or *Dark* (5%-10%), *Color* (10%-15%), and *Negro* or Black (more than 15%). The *Lágrima* type, as mentioned above, is made entirely from free-run juice; if aged for more than two years it may take on the appellative of *Lacrymae Christi*.

Finally, the Sierras de Málaga designation contemplates elegant white wines that are light straw in color and fresh and fruity in taste with tart overtones, and robust, well-structured red wines, with characteristic mineral bouquets and flavors.

Montilla-Moriles The Cordovan wines have been—and quite rightly—held in high esteem since time immemorial. This D.O. groups wines vinified from grapes cultivated on the calcareous soils of the Sierra de Montilla y Moriles in the territories of Aguilar de la Frontera, Lucen, Cabra, Doña Manía, and Puente Gentil and matured (mainly using the solera system) in oaken casks of maximum 1000-liter capacity in the southern part of the province of Córdoba. At 300-600 meters above sea level, the production zone is characterized by an extreme Mediterranean climate with continental influences and considerable rainfall, short, cold winters, and hot, dry summers. The predominant grape variety is the Pedro Ximénez, or better, Pero Ximén: it is said that this was the name of a foot-soldier in the Spanish Regiments serving in Flanders in the 16th century, who returned home bringing with him the vine that has taken his name. Besides this grape, the D.O. also accepts lesser percentages of the Airén, Baladí, Moscatel, and Torrontés varieties. Both the types and the styles are similar to those of the Jerez wines. We thus have dry types like the *fino* (14-17.5% alcohol), light in color with slightly bitter overtones and a hint of almond in the bouquet, and the aromatic *amontillado* (16-22%), with a nutty aroma and amber or old gold color, which is matured at least 2 years. The *ruedo* type is light in color, not aged, and contains a minimum of 14% alcohol.

Going on to the sweeter wines, we have the velvety, aromatic *oloroso*; aging can raise the alcohol content from 16-18% to 20%, and also darken the lovely mahogany color; the *palo cortado* (16-18% alcohol), similar in bouquet to the *amontillado* and in flavor to the *oloroso* (16-18%); and the *raya* (16-20%), similar to the *oloroso* but with a more delicate bouquet and flavor. The naturally-sweet Pedro Ximénez type is a resplendent ruby color that tends to darken with time.

White wines to be drunk young, aged for a maximum of one year, are also produced in the D.O. zone; they are delicate, light-colored, and fruity, with 10-13% alcohol-by-volume. The dry wines are ideal as apéritifs and are magnificent with ham and salami (even the smoked types). The sweet wines are obviously for dessert and sipping or "conversation" and "meditation" wines. 1990 and 1991 are considered excellent vintages, while 1989, 1992, 1994 and 1997 are considered very good.

The *bodegas* of Jerez and Málaga also mature excellent brandies (mainly by the solera system). There are also the strong *aguardientes* made by traditional methods: those of Ojén, in the province of Málaga, are especially renowned. Traditional alcoholic drinks include the *licores*, produced by slow maceration according to ancient recipes, and the *anisados* of Rute (Córdoba); Cazalla de la Sierra (Sevilla) produces aromatic *anisados* according to a peculiar method that has spread to other localities. Other excellent, traditionally-made liquors are to be found in the provinces of Huelva and of Sevilla, where cherries are transformed into the delicious *crema de guindas* cordial.

Where there's wine there's vinegar: Andalusia, which is certainly no exception to the rule, produces aromatic vinegars aged at length in oaken casks; the refined Jerez vinegar is probably the most famous.